Contents

Introduction

Marshalling writers into groups is always arbitrary. The cautious commentator realises this, and realises also that his personal opinions will inevitably involve now omissions, now truncations of others' favourite authors and themes. This is unavoidable in a book which aims both to give a general account of the period's novels, and to talk closely about selected individual novels; I hope that my eclecticism is a sign not of randomness but of flexibility.

In the following chapters my aim is to lead the reader in the right directions, not to define absolutely or dogmatise. When I have grouped authors together I have tried to remember how arbitrary such groupings are and how much of the distinct quality of the novel in any period rests not only on the interweaving and recurrence of certain common causes and characteristics, but on the individual works of individual authors.

However, some preliminary explanation is necessary for the omission of one or two writers who are chronologically on the border line and might just as well be discussed here, rather than in an earlier volume. Sherwood Anderson, whose classic *Winesburg, Ohio* appeared in 1919; Willa Cather, who produced *My Ántonia* in 1918, and, of course, Sinclair Lewis, with *Main Street* (1920), *Babbitt* (1922) and *Dodsworth* as late as 1929, could all fall within the scope of this survey of the twentieth-century novel. The reasons for their omission are partly pragmatic – the post-

1918 period is crammed full of interesting authors and, to allow space for them, borderline cases have been banished to the other side of the fence. A more serious excuse is to be found in the 'feel' of their books which makes them more pre- than post-Fitzgerald. In different ways they all look backwards. Willa Cather was over forty when her first novel was published, and was at her best as a historical novelist – *My Ántonia* takes a long nostalgic look into life in nineteenth-century Nebraska; Sherwood Anderson, for all his influence on Ernest Hemingway and William Faulkner, belongs to the older realistic-cum-naturalistic tradition of Theodore Dreiser – there is an almost deliberate quaintness about the provincialism of *Winesburg, Ohio* which bespeaks the presence of old nightmares seen in an old way (from Scott Fitzgerald on, the same nightmares are portrayed very differently). And Sinclair Lewis's work continually shows a harking backwards – he repeatedly finds himself in love with the very small-townishness that he set out to satirise as antiquated and damaging. In an equally recessive way, he could never bring himself to recognise, in his novels at least, that the clash was there.

Now to turn to the question of the traditional novel: while the heading of my first chapter is deliberately loose – to suggest certain possibilities to the reader rather than define for him – some introduction is needed, particularly since the chapter deals with Fitzgerald, Hemingway, Thomas Wolfe, John Dos Passos and John Steinbeck – a motley collection who seem only disparately related to a very notional tradition.

Yet they are traditional in at least two senses. First, they concern themselves with themes traditionally associated with the American novel in the nineteenth century: the wildness of the continent, whether natural or industrial, and the isolation of the individual in the face of it; the special problems of the relationship between individual and society in a country which has set myths about both; the passion for movement where there is so much country to move in; the sense of cultural inferiority *vis-à-vis*

Europe, coupled with the belief that there is something wrong about such feelings, that America must find and celebrate its own American culture – all of those themes common to the American novel before 1918, common to Hermann Melville, Nathaniel Hawthorne, Henry James, Upton Sinclair and Dreiser, find new expression in Fitzgerald, Hemingway, Dos Passos, Wolfe and Steinbeck.

'New expression' is, however, the key term here. For in each of these writers we find the same realisation which was striking their foreign contemporaries – namely, that a fundamental change was taking place, that things were not quite the same any more. Yet one of the oddities of fundamental change is that it is hard to identify precisely or even to describe. Was World War I, for example, a cause of fundamental change or the manifestation of a great altering process in behaviour and attitudes that was already under way? The question is a vast one, but the only aspect of it that concerns us here is how conscious these authors were that something had happened and that the traditional concerns of the American writer were, intangibly perhaps, to be played out in a new way. No doubt the war itself had something definite to do with this, for it opened America to the world and the world to America in a way that was not previously the case. It was not only that crowds of American servicemen who had never been outside their home states saw Europe for the first time; it was not just that 'educated' Americans who had been raised on a species of ersatz European culture came suddenly in touch with the real thing; it was the realisation that America was now not *at* the centre of things (which had originally been James's hope for it) but was the centre of things itself. The old European order was breaking up, entering a period of bewildering mutation, and it was now America which had the economic, the social and perhaps even the emotional power to hold up and lead Western civilisation. In a real sense it was America which had won that war, not merely in the sense that her troops had ultimately tipped the balance but that she alone gained from it, while all the European powers, victors and vanquished alike, were horribly damaged.

I am aware of the danger of historical generalisations, all the more so when they are wrapped around authors' works, yet surely we can see in Fitzgerald, Hemingway and the rest a new attitude to America, a carrying over of traditional American themes into a wider sphere. For American problems are no longer solely American – what were once America's local problems have become the world's.

Naturally cultural changes of this magnitude do not happen in an instant; the American author putting pen to paper on Armistice Day 1918 did not suddenly find his whole perspective altered. Yet the writers discussed in my first chapter do show a gradual altera- tion in attitude – principally towards the universality of their own American experience. In short, they show a movement away from the provincial to the universal.

This last point is a contentious one. It is almost a critical commonplace (among American critics as well as European ones) that the American writer in the 1920s is a provincial fellow, happy when he can rush off to Europe, happiest when he can go back home and brag to the boys in the back room about how swell it all was. The charge has been levelled at Fitzgerald and Heming- way especially, but also at Henry Miller, Faulkner, Nathanael West and even at Dos Passos. Wide currency is given to the belief that each of them was a man who, accustomed to picking his nose, finds himself in proud but uneasy possession of a silk handkerchief. Leslie Fiedler writes:

> . . . the writers who came of age in the First World War remained what they were to begin with: country boys perpetually astonished at meeting the Big City and the Great World, provincials for ever surprised to discover themselves in London or Paris or Antibes, and afterwards dazzled to remember that they had ever been in such improbable places.

They were, in short, 'provincial tourists'.

This attitude involves a misunderstanding of provincialism. The true provincial is the man who holds that his own limited experience is limitless, who claims that his own small world is superior to the greater one which lies outside it. Yet this is really not the attitude of Hemingway or Fitzgerald; they neither reject Europe as ridiculously inflated and over-praised compared to the true homey grit of Mother America nor do they use their own European experience to patronise America and American values. Of course, they had the imagination to be impressed with Europe but they do not stand about gaping. Perhaps an even more telling point is the way they treat provincialism itself; they realise there is a provincial vein in any exile, that Americans are often accused of a raw parochialism, and they look at these matters dead-on without the hysteria or the aversion which would immediately argue the truth of the charge.

People who are conscious of the charge of provincialism and able to consider it intelligently are no longer provincial. One of the most characteristic signs of the American novel from 1920 on is its gradual freedom to explore local American experiences, or the experiences of local Americans, as universal. In *The Sun Also Rises* (or *Fiesta* as it is alternatively entitled) Hemingway drew up a cast list of Americans and Europeans whose problems were held entirely in common and which owed absolutely nothing to European patronising or an American sense of inferiority. Fitzgerald, who was far more concerned with the seismic signals of society's behaviour, viewed provincialism with a deadly even-handedness, condemning the would-be sophisticated provincialism of the rich, whether European or American; more than that, Dos Passos and Faulkner made a valid distinction between the local and the provincial. 'I discovered,' says Faulkner, 'that my own little postage stamp of native soil was worth writing about and that I would never live long enough to exhaust it.' Now writing should 'attempt to cut a swathe through the American jungle without the use of a European compass'. Now the American novel could do what only the very great writers of the previous century had achieved and with the greatest difficulty – not only use local American experience as universal but do so instinctively, without the nagging doubt that, after all, it might be a provincial presumption.

The novelists of my first chapter, then, are traditional in at least two senses: they adapt areas of interest traditional to the American novel of the past, and they incorporate a sense of extended universal possibility for American fiction that, in its turn, provides a sense of solidity and authority towards which later writers, of all nationalities, may react. In a way, what they do is to bring about an accepted extension in the scale and scope of American fiction, and to allow the American writer to make the same assumptions that every writer who wishes to attempt great things must be able to make – that his own experience is valuable and the only thing standing between him and its successful portrayal is his own personality, his own talent.

CHAPTER 1

The Traditional Novel

F. SCOTT FITZGERALD

It is hard to read Fitzgerald's novels without thinking of the man himself, the Fitzgerald of legend whose double-breasted, straw-hatted figure stands woozily but obstructively between us and his books. The facts of his life have been over-popularised. The mixture of Southern and Irish in his make-up, his erratic career at Princeton, the immediate success of his first novel, the wildly disastrous marriage to Zelda, the enormous consumption of money and liquor, his alcoholism, Zelda's insanity, his work in Hollywood as a screen hack, his tragic and early death – it all reads very like a novel. Yet readers of the two admirable biographies of Fitzgerald will find the vulgar jazz-age image inadequate. Although Scott Fitzgerald had his problems, his work is distinguished not by its modishness, not by its rising and falling on a tide of self-indulgence, but by the most ancient of themes – struggle – applied to the most modern of subjects – the collapse of the individual.

Fitzgerald's established reputation as one of the most important novelists of twentieth-century America rests not so much on the creation of several individual masterpieces as on the talent he manifests in a limited number of flawed but fascinating works. This may in part be due to the extremely high standard of achievement he attained in his short stories – even up to the late Pat Hobby stories that he himself despised as potboilers; these reflect an exceptional power of expression and control of form which absorbed much of his creative energy. However, it is novels not short stories that concern us here and in that area Fitzgerald's output is brilliantly uneven.

His first two novels – the fashionable *This Side of Paradise* (which gained him instant commercial success) and *The Beautiful and Damned* – are broadly similar. Each is a *Bildungsroman* describing the education and development of a particularly charming, spoilt, egotistical, lazy and talented young man who journeys through a series of disillusionments about America until he arrives at some notional self-awareness.

The weaknesses of these novels are very much the weaknesses of their heroes, whose self-condemnation is just as narcissistic as their earlier self-praise and who are altogether too eager to heap the blame for their own failures on to the American social system. Understandably both novels are generally regarded as immature portrayals of immaturity. The weaknesses are well known, yet the books do contain features which prefigure Fitzgerald's later work.

Both novels deal with the respective heroes' attraction to and repulsion from glamour; indeed Amory Blaine and Anthony Patch are revolted partly by the very fact that they are and can be so attracted. The novels show a world of relationships which, like Amory's, disintegrate at a touch or, like Anthony's with Gloria, were never really there in the first place and are maintained as a desperate façade. Each novel deals with sexual revulsion. Witness Amory Blaine on kissing:

... their lips brushed like young flowers in the wind.
    'We're awful,' rejoiced Myra gently. She slipped her hand into his, her head drooped against his shoulder. Sudden revulsion seized Amory, disgust, loathing for the whole incident. He desired frantically to be away, never to see Myra again, never to kiss any-

one; he became conscious of his face and hers, of their clinging hands, and he wanted to creep out of his body ...

Even more striking are the several scenes of revulsion in *The Beautiful and Damned*. On the night before his wedding, Anthony is wakened in 'aversion and horror' by the noise of two people copulating: 'Life was that sound out there, that ghastly reiterated female sound.' In a similar and even more hysterical scene Gloria, lying down in her room during a party, sees (or imagines she sees – the point is obscure) a drunken house guest called Hull in her bedroom doorway. Although he walks away she rushes out of the house and engages in a sort of weird nocturnal cross-country run away from 'an indescribable and subtly menacing terror, a personality filthy, under its varnish, like smallpox spots under a layer of powder'. She is obviously running, in part at least, from her own feelings about sex. In another, better-known scene Anthony sees the devil as a result of allowing his inattentive head to fall upon a prostitute's shoulder!!

These sexual problems are merely a specific symptom of the general malaise which these two early novels set out to depict – that contemporary American society is in a state of dislocation and disintegration where the young, in the absence of any convincing moral system, have nothing to do but move faster and faster. Here is Amory articulating the philosophy of the young:

'I loathed the army. I loathed business. I'm in love with change and I've killed my conscience' –
'So you'll go on crying that we must go faster?'
'That at least is true,' Amory insisted.

It is a philosophy which is given more mature consideration in Fitzgerald's spectacularly talented yet still curiously limited *The Great Gatsby*. As Maxwell Geismar writes:

... after these lovely dying cadences which bring the novel to its full stop, why do we, all the same, have another and different sense of loss – that this novel, which is so good, could not have been just a little better?

A long analysis of *The Great Gatsby* has been done elsewhere; in what is one of the most carefully planned novels of the century, there is ample profit in that kind of investigation for critic and student alike. Some understanding is necessary, however, of how close it comes to being *the* American novel. The reason is obvious: *The Great Gatsby* concentrates with the utmost intensity on the greatest American myth – that America is a place where dreams come true. Of course, it is currently fashionable to sneer at the whole notion of 'the American dream', to point out the absurdity of accepting the fairy tales propagated by Horatio Alger and his ilk, to demonstrate that for every barefoot boy who becomes a millionaire at least a hundred remain barefoot, that for each individual who strives and succeeds a hundred strive only to fail. Yet this is only one side of the story. For, whatever fashion says, America is certainly a country where – to put it at the very least – dreams sometimes come true, and that 'sometimes' is enough to inspire, indeed to fire, a national imagination. In order for the American dream to become a cliché, it had first to possess a considerable foundation in fact. It is vital to remember that the social clamour raised by reforming novelists involves not a bald rejection of the dream but, for the most part, a demand that it be made real for everybody – and sometimes even more than that, to allow the dream to *continue* to be real. In Steinbeck's *Grapes of Wrath* all the Joad family want is to get back what they always had – their farm and the sense of independence and dignity that came from working it. In America, precisely because the dream can be real, why should anyone who is prepared to work be excluded from it?

The significance of work is considerable. It is interesting that one of the standard arguments used against negroes was not that they did not have dreams but that they were too lazy to put them into effect. The same argument has continually been used against the unsuccessful in America – they just plain couldn't have worked hard enough. This attitude could only have the force it does amongst otherwise intelligent and sensible people because so much success *has* been gained by striving.

Thus there grows up a special relationship between dreams and reality – a relationship peculiar to America. The consciousness of the dream is everywhere coupled with the possibility as well as the necessity of making it reality. Originally a man had to put the dream into action or go under. In the puritan communities of colonial days the whole society existed to make an ideal a reality. Similarly, when the settlers went west, the physical odds against them were too heavy to admit of non-commitment: you worked hard, very hard, or you died. It was as simple as that – and one of the factors motivating the 'social' novelist from Upton Sinclair onwards was that it isn't as simple as that any more.

In *The Great Gatsby*, however, Fitzgerald is engaged in a more subtle handling of America and its dream. For he is dealing with the effect that *consciousness* of the dream has upon individuals, and the break-up taking place in American society which invalidates the old relationship between dream and reality.

Although Gatsby himself represents the most obvious example of the effect of dream on consciousness, that effect applies to all the characters in *The Great Gatsby* and it is perhaps a sign of the novel's subtlety that this is not more immediately striking – it not only affects the characters but informs the whole atmosphere.

Most of the characters, except Gatsby and the Wilsons, are in a sense the inheritors of the dream made reality. Nick's family owns a profitable hardware business in the West, and Nick himself is being supported by his father while he goes East and learns ' "the bond business. Everybody I knew was in the bond business, so I supposed it could support one more single man." ' It is easy to be caught up in the extravagance of Gatsby's fall and overlook Nick's attitude, and nowhere is it easier than in his attitude to money:

> I bought a dozen volumes on banking and credit and investment securities, and they stood on my shelf in red and gold like new

money from the mint, promising to unfold the shining secrets that only Midas and Morgan and Maecenas knew.

In a pleasant, lackadaisical way Nick is cashing in on the act, taking what other people's dreams have provided, without any particular thrust or vision or ideal of his own, without any consideration of morals. Nick is using dreams, just as are Tom and Daisy, who come from similar backgrounds. The similarity in background between Nick and Tom is frequently stressed in the novel, thereby making a point that might otherwise be overshadowed by the difference in the amount of wealth of their respective families.

Tom does not know what to do with his time or his money or himself; he is deracinated, and a measure of the distance between him and the actual source of his money is the extraordinary way in which he looks at America. ' "Civilisation's going to pieces," broke out Tom violently. "I've gotten to be a terrible pessimist about things." ' As the novel goes on, this view of Tom's, which at first appears to be a subject for family/dinner/party amusement, becomes all too serious. Clearly, as his attitude towards Daisy and Gatsby shows, civilisation – and particularly American civilisation – simply means that which Tom owns, and any amount of dishonest self-justification will do, so long as it continues the owning process. There is also something particularly competitive about this ownership, a competitiveness that is in Tom a weird and twisted offshoot of the great tree of the American dream. Tom is created to compete, to fight, to struggle and win, and when this is denied its natural social outlet it becomes the force with which – to use Fitzgerald's terms – you smash up things and creatures.

On this topic an interesting comparison can be made between Tom and Meyer Wolfsheim on the one hand, and Gatsby on the other. Wolfsheim is the creator of Gatsby's wealth; ironically (the whole novel is a web of ironies) Wolfsheim uses Gatsby not only in the financial sense as a front man but also as an ideal, in very much the same way as Gatsby uses Daisy, and for that matter as everyone uses Gatsby. Gatsby is Wolfsheim's American dream. ' "I made him," says Wolfsheim to Nick, " . . . I raised him up out of nothing, right out of the gutter. I saw right away that he was a fine-appearing, gentlemanly young man, and when he told me he was an Oggsford I knew I could use him good." ' But there too is the difference between Wolfsheim's dream and Gatsby's – and indeed between Gatsby and the other characters. For to Wolfsheim the limit of a dream is its usefulness; it is a nice thing to have while it serves your own interests, a nice thing to reminisce about after the event. To Gatsby the dream of Daisy is worth taking blame for, suffering for and ultimately dying for. There is a medieval courtesy about Gatsby's dream, a fact that is all the more affecting when we realise that it did not start like that. Originally '. . . he made the most of his time. He took what he could get ravenously and unscrupulously – eventually he took Daisy one still October night, took her because he had no real right to touch her hand.' It didn't work out like that because 'he felt married to her, that was all' – and married to her is how he behaves. And the consequence of *that* is the moral and spiritual limitlessness of Gatsby's dream. In fact, by another irony, although Daisy herself turns out worthless, Gatsby's is the only dream in the novel that can come true, in the profound and serious sense in which it was first intended. It is this fact that makes Nick's last words to Gatsby valid: ' "They're a rotten crowd," I shouted across the lawn. "You're worth the whole damn bunch put together." ' For, despite Gatsby's bootlegging, his intermittent lying, his vulgarity, his is the only American dream in the novel – because it's married to something, that's all.

Caught up in the atmospheric splendour of *The Great Gatsby*, it is easy to miss how specifically Fitzgerald wishes us to relate these concerns to America as a whole, and especially to the relation between its Eastern and Western parts. In the last pages Nick says:

'I see now that this has been a story of the West, after all – Tom and Gatsby, Daisy and Jordan and I, were all Westerners, and perhaps

we possessed some deficiency in common which made us subtly
unadaptable to Eastern life.'

It is interesting that Fitzgerald includes that 'after all', for if we
make a list of the references to East versus West it turns out to be
considerable indeed, and it is a sign of the subtlety with which
issues are presented that this one is not obtrusive. The novel
begins with Nick's return to the West after the whole Gatsby
episode (which is told in flashback) – a return which implies, and
this is later confirmed, a rejection of the East's moral values. One
thing we learn very quickly is that in the West families matter;
Nick has a close relationship with his father, and it is a collective
family decision that Nick should come East and learn the bond
business. The contrast between Daisy's attitude as a parent –
gushing, affected and semi-detached from her child – is obvious.

From this beginning the novel is peppered with East-West contrasts. When Nick goes to dine *chez* Tom and Daisy it is the West
that they talk about – a West that they have all left with self-
conscious and restless sophistication; and we gradually see that the
West is an implied standard, that all the gorgeous and non-
sensical extravagance could not happen there. Going to New
York, crossing Queensborough Bridge, Nick and Gatsby are
passed by two highly contrasting groups: the first is an immigrant
funeral procession – the mourners 'looked out at us with the
tragic eyes and short upper lips of south-eastern Europe'; and the
second

> . . . a limousine . . . driven by a white chauffeur, in which sat three
> modish Negroes, two bucks and a girl. I laughed aloud as the
> yolks of their eyeballs rolled toward us in haughty rivalry.
>   'Anything can happen now that we've slid over this bridge,' I
> thought; 'anything at all . . .'
>   Even Gatsby could happen, without any particular wonder.

The point being made here is the contrast between one's sense
of wonder at the mad chaos of contemporary civilisation – a

helpless and despairing wonder – and what ought to be the real sense of wonder at America, 'the first wild promise of all the mystery and beauty in the world'. The latter sense of wonder, the genuine American wonder, is found, Fitzgerald suggests, only in the West.

This suggestion is evident at the end of the novel, in the section where Nick describes his past homecomings:

> Even when the East excited me most, even when I was most keenly aware of its superiority to the bored, sprawling, swollen towns beyond the Ohio, with their interminable inquisitions which spared only the children and the very old – even then it had always for me a quality of distortion.

The 'superiority' of the East that Nick feels consists in its excitement, its cosmopolitanism, its sophistication and above all its aesthetic sense. An Eastern dinner party, for example, is 'sharply different from the West, where an evening was hurried from phrase to phrase towards its close, in a continually disappointed anticipation or else in sheer nervous dread of the moment itself'.

But the West, lacking these qualities, possesses moral standards which the East cannot equal; its dreams, like Gatsby's, are married to something.

Some readers react violently to this attitude of Fitzgerald's, pointing out that his East-West antithesis is too generalised, his condemnation of the East far too sweeping and that he lets the West much too easily off the hook. Are there not, they say, ash pits and poor in the West; is the East entirely without principles, and can one section of the country be held responsible for the corruption of the other?

But this is to make Fitzgerald appear altogether too systematic a novelist; his concern is with turning ideas over, with bringing issues into our consciousness, rather than in tying reef-knots in social ropes. It is possible then to see the East-West antithesis as a focus for bringing certain facts about America and its dream to our attention – facts which Fitzgerald clearly saw as of burning and immediately contemporary importance. He was worried about the way America was going, that the American dream could become the American nightmare. He saw in the West the possibilities – perhaps no more than that – of the former; in the East the coming threat of the latter.

This can be seen in the last view that Nick has of the East. Before leaving for home he goes down to the beach by Gatsby's house and imagines:

> . . . the old island here that flowered once for Dutch sailors' eyes – a fresh, green breast of the new world . . . for a transitory enchanted moment man must have held his breath in the presence of this continent, compelled into an aesthetic contemplation he neither understood nor desired, face to face for the last time in history with something commensurate to his own capacity for wonder.

It is not just the East, part or whole, that is so beautifully evoked there, it is 'this continent', America, and there is no better description of the sheer scale of the aspirations it arouses than in the last sentence of that quotation.

On that same last page Fitzgerald pushes home the dangers of the present time. He introduces another sense of wonder – Gatsby's.

> He had come a long way to this blue lawn, and his dream must have seemed so close that he could hardly fail to grasp it. He did not know that it was already behind him, somewhere back in that vast obscurity beyond the city, where the dark fields of the republic rolled on under the night.

The dark fields of the republic *rolling* on, and at night, recall Nick's train journey home – home to the West; and it is significant that Nick's journey is the only other part of the book where the country (not just the countryside) is evoked with the tenderness and beauty of the Dutch sailors' sighting of the East. One may think therefore that Fitzgerald is suggesting some salvation as possible for the East if it can recover the feeling for the country, the sense of wonder spawned by the past that still has some actual existence in the West. Similarly we may see a suggestion that Gatsby's dream took the wrong turning – that it should have stayed at home where it had a chance. And perhaps we may also feel the presence of a warning: America's future can only lie in its past – in dreams that are married to things – and the section of America that forgets that is a section doomed.

The Great Gatsby then is *the* novel of the American dream; yet, although the statement is undoubtedly true, having made it one is forced to pause for a moment and wonder why. After all, since the notion of the American dream is so widespread, indeed endemic, it follows that there are countless novels which touch upon it and a great many that concentrate on it entirely. So what is so special about Fitzgerald? Is it merely a matter of talent? And is Fitzgerald's talent so much greater than, say, Wolfe's or Dos Passos' or Jack Kerouac's?

Talent may have something to do with it, but there is a more likely explanation, which goes some way towards solving Maxwell Geismar's problem about the surprising limitations of the novel. For the great achievement, and possibly also the great limitation, of the book is that everything in it is dreamlike. There has rarely been a novel in which the theme is so perfectly reflected in the texture of the work. The sequence of events, the prose, the very presentation of the characters, all have a dreamlike quality. The combination of these facts explains why so short a novel creates so intense an effect. It is an achievement of the sort that one normally associates with poetry – it is not surprising that Fitzgerald saw his own talent as being of an essentially poetic kind. Reading *Gatsby* is at times like reading Wordsworth, where a remembered scene has the combined distinctness and indistinctness that we associate with a dream. Certain central features stand out with spectacular vividness, with a spectacularly *selected* vividness, while in the background and on the perimeter other features show themselves shadowy, muzzily blurred.

It is easy to see how this would be advantageous in a novel about dreams, but why it should also be a limitation is less obvious. First, and least, for it occurs infrequently, there is an occasional trancelike, almost sleep-walking wooziness about the prose.

> Through all he said, even through his appalling sentimentality, I was reminded of something – an elusive rhythm, a fragment of lost words, that I had heard somewhere a long time ago. For a moment a phrase tried to take shape in my mouth, and my lips parted like a dumb man's, as though there was more struggling upon them than a wisp of startled air. But they made no sound, and what I almost remembered was uncommunicable forever.

Another problem consists in a certain incompatibility between the novel's dreamlike quality and its moral stance. 'When I came back from the East last autumn I felt that I wanted the world to be in uniform and at a sort of moral attention forever.' The morality which Fitzgerald is offering – vague though it may be – has an edge of Western breeze about it and a lump of Western backbone. But how constructive and useful is it? It may be all right for Nick who can retreat to 'the Carraway house in a city where dwellings are called through decades by a family's name' – but what about people who do not have that (presumed) moral advantage; what about the Wilsons of this world; what about the people who do not come from the West at all, and for that matter what about those features of the West that created Gatsby out of Gatz and set him on the path to destruction? It is all too indistinct, and reflects an ambivalence on Fitzgerald's part. His morality and his powers of observation do not quite fit, and in order to make them fit he forces them.

That is evident also in his treatment of Gatsby, with whom he clearly sympathises. In order to correct too favourable an impression – for after all Gatsby is a crook, and a crook who, whether by commission or omission, still ruins people – Nick throws in the odd comment about disapproval. But while it is easy to accept that Nick at times looks down on Gatsby in a snobbish way, the idea that his disapproval is moral is much harder to take.

It is important, however, to realise that the impression produced by this sort of thing is less one of contradiction than one of vagueness; it, in fact, contributes to the dream-texture of the novel. The same point applies to his treatment of characters, who are bound up in and restricted by the needs of the texture. (In this respect Fitzgerald is very much the heir of Henry James.) His description of Daisy provides a good example:

> I looked back at my cousin, who began to ask me questions in her low, thrilling voice. It was the kind of voice that the ear follows up and down, as if each speech is an arrangement of notes that will never be played again. Her face was sad and lovely with bright things in it, bright eyes and a bright passionate mouth, but there was an excitement in her voice that men who had cared for her found difficult to forget . . .

As introduction to and a preparation for an understanding of the character, that is very good; it makes us want to know more – but we find out hardly any more about Daisy. It is true we learn that she is weak and a liar, but there is always an indistinct, a blurry quality about her – and indeed about all the characters. It is not merely that they exist only to fulfil such demands as the author may make upon them – that, after all, is true of many authors – but that the specific demand Fitzgerald is making is that they should merge into the strange shadowy world of the dream: Gatsby's world.

There is, however, one more point worth making about Daisy, a point partly suggested by the 'bright passionate mouth' and 'excitement in her voice' of that last quotation: how successfully does Fitzgerald portray female sexuality? The question might be irrelevant in many cases; after all, how many of the great novelists portray sexuality at all, never mind successfully? But here it is important because Daisy's sexuality is seen by Fitzgerald as being curiously horrifying. The Daisy who – presumably because of her love for Gatsby – has to get drunk the night before her marriage is radiantly transformed by the honeymoon. Says Jordan Baker, 'I've never seen a girl so mad about her husband.' Given Tom's absolute lack of kindness, Daisy's devotion can only be sexual. While Fitzgerald treats this very lightly, he obviously sees Daisy's transference from Gatsby to Tom then back again to Gatsby as an indication of the same selfish rapacity he saw elsewhere in Tom and Wolfsheim. Despite the circumstances of her seduction it is she, not Gatsby, who is rapacious. Yet to many readers it appears that Daisy is being blamed not for the fickleness of her sexual feelings but simply for having sexual feelings in the first place. This hardly seems fair, and what we encounter here is something that vitiates Fitzgerald's longer novel, *Tender Is The Night* – namely, his determination to seek out moral scapegoats. The last quarter of *Tender Is The Night* invites us to identify increasingly with Dick Diver's self-pity and to heap a particularly grudge-ridden burden of blame on the rich for decisions that he supposedly took freely and with full knowledge.

'If he could write a book as fine as *The Great Gatsby* I was sure he could write an even better one,' – yet most critics would agree with Hemingway's subsequent judgement that Fitzgerald never actually superseded *Gatsby*. His achievement is still considerable, extending through the great mass of his short stories and the (equally) dreamlike *Tender Is The Night* to the tragically unfinished *Last Tycoon* – all meriting as much attention as we have given to his other work. The achievement is varied; however, one central point can be made here, and it is simply that Fitzgerald is *new*. The issues that he outlines – and principally the individual locked in a struggle for survival – may be as old as literature itself but their context is unmistakably novel. In a sense, therefore, Fitzgerald makes the twentieth-century American novel possible, for he shows that the twentieth century is here and America must learn to make the best of it, and American literature the best *with* it. Amory Blaine, Anthony Patch and Gatsby are all characters caught up in the problem of what America is to become and of what is to become of America; of how the American past can serve in the creation of a new and violently modern present.

ERNEST HEMINGWAY

There are authors about whom it is hazardous not to take sides – the 'fors' and the 'againsts' being so vehement and vicious. Hemingway is one of these. There are other writers about whom it is equally dangerous to express a moderate opinion – the two extremes attacking you for not being 'proish' or 'connish' enough. Hemingway is one of these too.

As in the case of Fitzgerald, this is not just a literary matter but a question of personality, a commodity which Hemingway possessed in public abundance. Hemingway boxing, Hemingway fishing, Hemingway war reporting, Hemingway shooting lions, Hemingway remembering what it was like being Hemingway a long time ago – there was always the publicity, the interest. The photographs too: the great head belligerent, the great body shrunken or expanded according to the amount eaten and drunk while fishing, war reporting, shooting lions; one can understand why his enemies felt that, if there had been no Hemingway, *Life* magazine would have been compelled to invent one. It is easy also to imagine why his worshippers worshipped. For, even if time has exposed some cracks in the armour of Hemingwayan truthfulness, he undoubtedly did a great many of the things he talked about; and he was certainly entitled to talk about violence – many types of which he had witnessed – and about the pain that he experienced all his life and bore with fortitude.

Of course, Hemingway's personality is not a matter to be settled, or even discussed, by the simple citing of antithetical positions. One of the most interesting side issues is the way in which Hemingway's personality cult shows America abandoning its provincialism and taking, or at very least sharing, the centre of the artistic stage. In Europe in the nineteenth century the artist, as a public figure, had assumed a personality role not conspicuously to be found in America. American artists before Hemingway, even if they were not universally shabby, certainly suffered from no great glare of publicity. Interest in their lives was largely a provincial matter; it was the bankers and soldiers and politicians, and the occasional figure floating upward from the (usually European) demi-monde who achieved the limelight. The very presence of Hemingway as a cult figure is a sign of America's increasing cosmopolitanism, as, for that matter, is Hemingway's unselfconscious setting of his novels abroad. If his Americans feel inferior, it is not for being American. Like the eighteenth- or nineteenth-century Englishman, the American is taking it for granted that he is at the centre of things, that *his* form of experience is completely valid and that, if anything, Europe should come to him rather than the reverse.

It is a testament to Hemingway's power – for good or ill – that certain kinds of situations, certain forms of expression came to be known as 'Hemingwayan'. Hemingwayan contrasts the brutality and cruelty of life with the sensitivity of man's inner nature; Hemingwayan shows man in a life of physical action fighting with a hostile universe; Hemingwayan has a hero that reflects this; a hero caught up in battles or their aftermaths, or a hero who is in a constant state of test. Hemingwayan, too, is the prose that describes the hero and his universe, prose that is itself best described as 'simplicity forced under enormous pressure out of complexity'. Hemingwayan is the poetic entity created from these parts, a tense emotional whole.

But again the term can be used pejoratively, amounting indeed to a term of abuse. Hemingwayan then describes a world of childish masculine attitudinising, a world of male chauvinist piggery with god-like men, submissive women and utopian sex between them. Hemingwayan is a world in which everything is supposedly seen directly and honestly but turns out to be saturated with self-deception; Hemingwayan is turning the universe into a place where a man 'ain't got a chance nohow' just so that Hemingway's fear of the world and conviction of his own weakness will be excused. Hemingwayan is the whole work that is wholly escapist.

My own view is somewhere between the two, a position which will emerge as less paradoxical when we look more closely at his novels and realise that Hemingway, like Fitzgerald, is predominantly a novelist of collapse.

But first for a general view of Hemingway's *oeuvre*, beginning with several magnificent short stories of which 'Indian Camp' and 'Up in Michigan' may be taken as typical. Stories of superb atmospheric texture, strange stories in which violence and horror of the most extreme kind are presented in the most peculiarly objective way. In 'Indian Camp' a doctor delivers an Indian woman of a baby by Caesarean section, with a jack-knife and without anaesthetic, while her invalid husband in the bunk above, unable to bear the screaming, cuts his head nearly off with a razor. The stories are filtered through the consciousness of Nick Adams, who is a child in 'Indian Camp', and with whose formation the stories deal, each one marking a different stage in his development. As Philip Young points out in his excellent study, in each of the stories Nick encounters and learns to deal – however desperately – with the facts of violence and pain and suffering. It is interesting to notice that each vital area of human life – birth, childhood, sex, friendship, death – is seen in those terms; in these stories, every one of these experiences is surrounded by a pain too horrible to be borne.

The careful monotony of the style is a sign of what has happened to the characters' nerves; numbness is like shock, a way of enduring the otherwise unendurable. It soon becomes apparent that each story involves an initiation on Nick's part into horrifying mysteries, and the evolution of a complex ritual 'whereby thinking can be stopped, the evil spirits placated and warded off'. This ritual may be related to something which Hemingway himself once said, that 'cowardice . . . is almost always simply a lack of ability to suspend the functioning of the imagination' – in other words, the rituals of drinking, sport, sex, sometimes even fighting, in which the Hemingway hero engages, are ways of stopping thinking about the terror, horror and violence underneath. The position of the Hemingway hero, therefore, is at best stoic; out of the struggle emerges a sense of dignity, nobility, achievement, strength, which gives life the only meaning it has.

The early stories are remarkable in several ways. The original collection (even though it omits the vital 'Up in Michigan') could almost be a novel, so great is its emotional and atmospheric coherence, so thoroughly does it treat the multiple wounds of Nick Adams. The collection provides a clear foretaste of the issues of his future novels, and illustrates their strengths and weaknesses. The principal strengths lie in the portrayal of pain, psychological as well as physical, the ability to make the reader feel exactly what this sort of suffering is like. Strong also is the prose, itself suggesting feelings held at a tangent to the facts they are experiencing. The weaknesses of the tales should also be pointed out; for example, they deal with only one emotion – pain. Also there is a tendency, both in the subject matter and the prose, towards over-sensitivity. Philip Young makes the point that 'Nick, far from being calloused, is an extremely sensitive, even an abnormally sensitive human being'. He is correcting the ridiculously naïve view that because Nick may be silent and tough and even inarticulate he is therefore a boor. At the same time there is, to take up Young's terms, a difference between 'sensitive' and 'abnormally sensitive' – a difference which makes Hemingway's early work even more limited and exclusive. One wonders whether Hemingway's view, as filtered through Nick, is that of a sensitive man in a harsh universe or of someone so hopelessly damaged that his world view cannot be taken seriously.

The Sun Also Rises (or *Fiesta*) and *A Farewell to Arms* are frequently taken as Hemingway's best novels. Particularly in the United States the view is that thereafter a certain decline sets in and, with the exception of *The Old Man and the Sea* which represents an isolated throwback to the old abilities, he never achieves the same clear consistency of success again.

The Sun Also Rises certainly has many advantages. First and foremost, like *Gatsby*, it is so exactly and thoroughly steeped in its immediate period that it cannot but appeal to *all* periods. Hemingway renders with great vividness 'the lost generation' – a group of café exiles, American and English, living in Paris. It is also plain from the reaction to the book that he was symbolising something for people who had never seen Paris or a café. Much of the response must have been due to a widespread contemporary sense of exile. The characters are all exiled from a series of things that are hinted at though never discussed. There is the war; they are all war casualties, even those who have not fought. The hero, Jake, is physically impotent through a war wound; the other characters are psychically impotent. None of them has the power to be fulfilled or happy and one of Hemingway's successes is that we gradually become aware of this as the book goes on. The characters cannot have satisfactory relationships with each other – Brett Ashley with her nervous public promiscuity is merely an obvious representative of a general case. Emotionally it takes two to tango, a fact that Hemingway is still, at this early stage, ready to portray, and the characters who cannot have relations with her suffer from the same malaise. The character of Robert Cohn, who has an affair with Brett and won't 'let go', is an interesting example. He hangs about against Brett's hints, her fiancé Mike's malice, and the mute disapproval of the impotent Jake, until

Brett's affair with the bullfighter Romero drives Robert into fights with Jake and Romero. Critics who point out the strange mass-impotence of the whole group cite the drunken complaisance of Mike, the pandering of Jake – who virtually procures Romero for Brett – and they sometimes forget Robert, with whom, significantly, the book begins.

A very good case could be made for him as the most important character in the book's treatment of impotence. Firstly his attachment to Brett is the last in a long series of failing attachments to women, and Hemingway is careful to point out his responsibility for these. Secondly, there is an unmanly hangdog quality about his attachment; he hangs on not positively to win Brett back but to wallow in his rejection. Thirdly, he tries to redeem his masculinity by something unchallenging because unfemale, something he knows he will win at – boxing. And it is interesting that what makes him eventually leave is not the ultimate rejection of Brett but his failure to subdue Romero by beating him up. He is absolutely impotent.

In this connection we should notice the significance of the group – a phenomenon which is important throughout Hemingway. The group, as Philip Young points out, has a code – certain things are 'done', others 'not done'. Robert's problem is that he does things that 'aren't done' and is therefore an outsider. Despite the pain caused by members to each other (principally by Brett), the group is something in which to shelter – in a hostile world, the security of companionship it offers is better than nothing. It is interesting that in later novels even this security is removed from Hemingway's world view. In *A Farewell to Arms* companionship cannot survive the fragmenting influence of war. The middle novellas – *Francis Macomber* and *To Have and Have Not* – show man as perilously isolated and continually double crossed. In *For Whom the Bell Tolls* some individuals within groups do their duty but others do not and the result again is break-up. *Across the River and Into the Trees* is one long grumble about how badly groups – and particularly the army – have treated the hero; and in *The Old Man and the Sea* the old man is utterly isolated except for the eventual help of the boy Manolito, hardly a group of any solidarity. Indeed the movement of Hemingway's work from *The Sun Also Rises* on is to isolate the individual absolutely, to give him nowhere to go but death. It is, whatever gestures he periodically makes towards apologia, to show man losing to a hostile universe.

In *The Sun Also Rises*, however, Hemingway manages to generate a feeling of real sadness in the group's attempts to stick together, to face the world. Indeed the sympathy readers often feel for Hemingway's characters is close to that felt for Fitzgerald's – they are all brave children nonchalantly holding hands and pretending not to be frightened of the thunderstorm.

The analogy can, of course, also be used the other way – against Hemingway – for brave children are not brave adults; certainly many readers have felt that the characters and their world view is simply too childish to be taken as representative in any adult sense. It is reasonable, therefore, to object, say, to Stuart Sanderson's comments on the following passage. It is a conversation between Jake and Brett as they drive through the Paris night.

'And there's not a damn thing we could do,' I said.
'I don't know,' she said. 'I don't want to go through that hell again.'
'We'd better keep away from each other.'
'But, darling, I have to see you. It isn't all that you know.'
'No, but it always gets to be.'
'That's my fault. Don't we pay for all the things we do though.'
She had been looking into my eyes all the time. Her eyes had different depths, sometimes they seemed perfectly flat. Now you could see all the way into them.
'When I think of the hell I've put chaps through. I'm paying for it all now.'

In one respect this dialogue is very good. It shows two people *not* talking about something. ' "It isn't all *that* you know" ' – that is, not just the fact that as soon as Brett and Jake get together an insoluble sexual situation develops. The fact that these outspoken people cannot speak out about their frustration and impotence shows how much it matters. However, Sanderson makes a larger claim for the passage – a claim which is a representative one for Hemingway's prose.

> It is reticent, allusive, leaves much half-said and more unsaid . . . It is a dramatist's technique, telescoping past time and action . . . we learn . . . that Jake has looked into Brett's eyes many times, has met various degrees of reservation there, and now sees her inmost feelings exposed quite unreservedly. All this Hemingway manages with the utmost economy, letting the reader see only what Jake sees at that moment, but also compelling him to feel all that Jake feels and has ever felt.

Now the passage is certainly reticent and allusive, but I dispute how much it leaves unsaid. The dialogue confirms what we know about the characters rather than implies or reveals new information. We know from Jake's earlier encounter with a prostitute that he is impotent, and from Brett's earlier behaviour in the café that she is a bitch. The point about the different depths in her eyes is again confirming something that we have already seen and is quite the opposite of 'reticent' or 'allusive', being totally explicit. Again it is questionable how satisfactory is Jake's view that he now sees her inmost feelings. After all, her comment about payment for putting chaps through hell is hardly profoundly revelatory and is again quite explicit – yet it seems so silly that one is inclined to take it as a sign not so much of her superficiality but that Jake has got things wrong. And indeed one of the novel's problems is that the style, instead of suggesting the possibility of a whole series of underlying motivations, sticks with surface explanations – sticks, in fact, at the level of the wound. It seems to me that the exact opposite of Sanderson's final statement is the case: we *don't* feel all that Jake feels and has

34

ever felt. We are confirmed in an opinion and impression we have already received, and that impression is a limited one.

We are already encountering one of Hemingway's greatest problems – a form of repetition that poses as original statement. All we know about the characters we learn in the opening chapters; what we are told is not much, and we are told no more thereafter. There is no pre-wound Jake. Here a comparison with Evelyn Waugh is interesting for he, like Hemingway, produced books with a definite emotional texture; in the case of *A Handful of Dust* this involves pain, and specifically the pain of being hopelessly and cruelly wounded – a wounding which brings emotional and physical frustration in its wake. Yet in Waugh's novel, although the characterisation is deliberately superficial, we know what the people were like before the wound, in fact, we understand their makeup and motivations. In Waugh's case also the characters wound each other – whereas, for Hemingway, the wound is totally external. The war, like the butler of detective fiction, did it; and, once that information is supplied, the reader is not supposed to bother with additional explanation or motivation.

This does tend (I would not put it any stronger) to weaken the representativeness of Hemingway's case. If we can take the novel as limited simply to a depiction of the 'lost generation' during a certain limited period, that is all right as far as it goes, but we must admit that it is not far. Equally it is hard to accept *The Sun Also Rises* purely on this level because of the very gifts that its author employs. His gifts imply more. The cosmopolitan Hemingway is present for the first time and he suggests, mainly by a sort of wry confidence, that he is producing a profound view of a complex world. And up to a point this suggestion is justified. In the scene between Brett and Count Mipopoulos, in the description of Jake's fishing trip, in the evocation of the fiesta itself, we are certainly given a fresh and very intense view of life – or rather *look* at life – for, when the intensity and freshness tempt us to go deeper, we find that Hemingway has decided to shut up shop.

The novel's most complete success is, therefore, on a technical level. Repeatedly in the novel, the style works; it is fresh, it describes originally, it makes you look at the world in another way. Its only real weakness, contained almost epigrammatically in the novel's last sentence, is that it is not a style for judgements or generalisations. Even here, however, it is difficult to separate technique from content, and the point should become clearer by a look at what is often thought to be Hemingway's other 'best' novel, *A Farewell to Arms*.

This book illustrates the first obvious example of strain between what we might call the small and the large Hemingways; the small Hemingway wants to create a brief poignant vignette of pain, the larger to produce an epic story on a grand scale.

Certain sections of the novel are magnificent. The war scenes, showing the individual caught in a web of confusion, horror and excitement are positively Tolstoyan.

> I started up the embankment, slipping in the mud. The drivers were ahead of me. I went up the embankment as fast as I could go. Two more shots came from the thick brush and Aymo, as he was crossing the tracks, lurched, tripped and fell face down. We pulled him down on the other side and turned him over. 'His head ought to be uphill,' I said. Piani moved him around. He lay in the mud on the side of the embankment, his feet pointing downhill, breathing blood irregularly. The three of us squatted over him in the rain. He was hit low in the back of the neck and the bullet had ranged upward and come out under the right eye. He died while I was stopping up the two holes. Piani laid his head down, wiped at his face with a piece of the emergency dressing, then let it alone.

That passage is statement of the kind that Hemingway could use so effectively and which compares with the personal battle experiences in *War and Peace*. The passage conveys simultaneously the individual obscenity of war authenticised by the fact that the person recording it has no time to suffer or interpret or do anything but factually list what happened. How well it works may be seen in the splendidly unselfconscious irony contained in the last sentence; the absolute simplicity of the language creates a vivid difference between Aymo alive (*his* head, *his* face) and Aymo dead (let *it* alone). It is in battle scenes, or scenes of a concomitant kind – Frederick's wounding, his escape from the battle, his escape with Catherine, Catherine's death in childbirth – that the book is at its best.

The flaws in the novel are as obvious as its virtues. A long time ago Edmund Wilson made the now representative observation that the characters were flat and conventionalised – a fact which does not help Hemingway's portrayal of their love affair. What is striking is not merely that the characters and their love are weakly portrayed but that they are utter artistic failures, of an order of failure which is at odds with the sections just praised and means that the quality of those sections is often overlooked. The childish crudity of Catherine's character; the continual (unspecified) success of her lovemaking with Frederick; the sheer volume of her Dickens-heroine prattle-prattle which inevitably lowers our opinion of Frederick – who is not so substantial that he can afford that – and which spreads an air of false poeticising over so much of the book, and particularly its world view – these faults loom large.

Robert Lewis points out, in mitigation of these criticisms, that the novel is narrated in retrospect, that we have Frederick Henry looking back at himself, that we are intended to see him describing his relationship with Catherine as in some respects unsatisfactory at the time. Lewis reads Henry's frequent 'thinking about things' as signs of an uneasiness about his love affair: 'Henry has attempted to reduce life to its lowest denominator . . . to make it thoughtless, to destroy consciousness and responsibility in a romantic, orgiastic dream.' In other words, we are intended to suppose that a good deal of the novel is ironic, and that Hemingway was successfully conscious that he was writing about an immature young man and a neurotic young woman – or, to put it another way, two neurotics.

That Lewis himself has some doubts about the artistic success of this may be seen by his reference to the technique of an 'unreliable narrator' as sometimes deceptive, and indeed his findings are not borne out by *A Farewell to Arms* itself. First, the technique of the 'two Henrys' makes things worse, not better. Instead of having a mature view of an immature past, we have one flat man looking at another. Secondly, the only difference effectively pointed out between the two Henrys consists not at all in any ironic or even newly-aware reappraisal of Catherine and their relationship but simply in the realisation that their idyllic happiness could not last, thus proving that happiness cannot last and that the world is a nasty place.

This criticism of the narrator's role speaks against the theory of the novel's technical complexity – a theory which still has some impressive backers.

> The novel has one stylistic innovation that is important to it. This is the use of an object, rain, in a way that cannot be called symbolic so much as portentous . . . what is new in *A Farewell to Arms* is the consistent use of rain as a signal of disaster . . . (used) simply as a subtle and unobtrusive device for unity.

I first read the novel when I was fifteen and Hemingway's use of rain appeared to me even at that age, as it does today, not only unsubtle and obvious but cheap. Since every time anything even mildly unpleasant happens to the characters it rains, I do not see how we can talk of the unobtrusive. And, while it is fair for Young to speak of unity (the introductory scene does indeed contain rain, pregnancy and death, echoes of which reverberate through the book till its end and Catherine's death) unity can be ineffective – a point often missed. In fact, the unity of *A Farewell to Arms* is so cheap and easy, so evades the novel's real areas of concern, so plugs into our easiest responses by obvious poeticism and romanticised suffering, that we may easily read in it the true beginning of Hemingway's artistic troubles – the self-indulgence, the wallowing in his own characteristics.

And yet ... when all that has been said, how well Hemingway gets away with certain things. The actual death of Catherine is good not only in the same way and for the same reasons as the death scene quoted earlier but because it comes very close to justifying its philosophic claims.

> Now Catherine would die. That was what you did. You died. You did not know what it was about. You never had time to learn. They threw you in and told you the rules and the first time they caught you off base they killed you. Or they killed you gratuitously like Aymo. Or gave you the syphilis like Rinaldi. But they killed you in the end. You could count on that. Stay around and they would kill you.

If ever there was a case for the implacable hostility of the universe it must surely come across in death in childbirth – of all deaths it seems the unfairest, and the more so in that so little could be done (then at least) to prevent it. And by showing such death so graphically Hemingway should surely win our emotional approval for his general case.

Should? ... obviously the extent to which he does win our approval must vary with the individual's response; but, if it doesn't succeed, it must be because Hemingway is not showing us individuals responding. He has given us not people but response-kits; where they collide with our own terrors the emotional force is considerable, but we know that they do not exist outside the operating theatre, and they certainly cannot sustain the demands made upon them by a novel of this scale. Oddly, what we are describing there is the problem of the failed epic novel, the same failure that applies to *For Whom the Bell Tolls*. Hemingway has the necessary narrative gift and the capacity for making his private scenes representational on a grand scale. But he cannot create people and, since the essence of the twentieth-century epic situation is how the individual rejects or is rejected by monolithic public/political norms, the presence of that gap is the measurement of Hemingway's epic failure.

It is this failure which we mark throughout the rest of Hemingway's career – a failure which increases in direct proportion to his indulgence of his hero. This indulgence takes two main and related forms: granting the character egregious achievements and producing some authorial comments that show him in an indulgently favourable light. The two coincide most disastrously in *Across the River and Into the Trees*, but there are decided manifestations of them in all the rest of his work – the sole exception being the remarkable *The Old Man and the Sea*.

An ardent Hemingwayan may seem to be mistaking potential for actual achievement, but that potential undoubtedly achieves its promise in *The Old Man and the Sea*. The objections which critics have raised do not sound convincing – provided one reads the tale as a work on its own, without any preconceptions either about Hemingway's own character or the central preoccupations consistently manifested in his other writing. The immense achievements of the work – once this is done – far overcome its liabilities. Literal objections (that the boy Manolito could not possibly carry heavy fishing equipment; that sharks could just as easily attack a boat in shallow as deep water – thus invalidating the judgement that Santiago 'went out too far', with all its obvious symbolism) do not strike us as we *read* the book. Similarly the boy's worship of the old man – 'redolent of [authorial] self-admiration' – creates quite a different impression if we rid our minds of preconceptions about the self-worship of earlier Hemingway heroes. If anyone ever did deserve a little hero-worship, it is the 'old man'. In other words, Hemingway has created a tale so convincing and gripping that minor exterior reservations vanish – we suspend our disbelief. The same point applies to the style: if we have no preconceptions, it works perfectly well.

For anyone who has not read *The Old Man and the Sea* it would be disastrous here to discuss it at length; the story is too briefly delicate to survive heavy analysis. It is necessary, however, to mention some of the attributes Hemingway displays in it. What in this context is immediately striking is the combination of narrative skill, the *rootedness* in character of the famous Hemingway features of simplicity, a symbolism that stretches out to universality, and a really successful treatment of pain. That Hemingway's central character is a peasant helps considerably; rightly or wrongly we are inclined to accept the rhythm of peasant lives as being close to the workings of the universe – indeed, almost a symbolic reflection of them. The same barriers do not exist in *The Old Man and the Sea* as elsewhere between Hemingway's character and the use to which he is put. Moreover the character of the old man is both wide enough to admit of universal significance and specific enough to exist as a person. Interesting in this connection is the treatment of Santiago's pain; not only is it less melodramatic than Jake's or Frederick Henry's but it occurs in context; we can see through the pain barrier to how *this* character reacts under pain, which makes his coping with it less isolated, less grandiose and more affirmative. The truth is that, of all Hemingway's central characters, Santiago alone has the dignity of a man – the rest have the dignity of ruined children. On the subject of the narrative power which unites with character I will only say that Hemingway achieves the great double desired by all writers of suspense: one longs to know what will happen next and prays that it will not hurt the character. This is partly due to Hemingway's superb gift for procedure; he could give a shopping list a sense of sequential suspense and thereby let the reader know exactly what being in the shop was like; this same gift is found in the best police procedural writers, like Ed McBain, and I would suggest that the influence of Hemingway on popular fiction – so often restricted to the phoney 'tough guy' response – may also be both benign and subtle.

I have earlier referred to the two Hemingways – the small and the large, the composer of the essay on pain, and the epic chronicler – and their failure to come satisfactorily together. It is ironic, therefore, that the closest Hemingway comes to overcoming that failure should be in this work, and on so small a scale. In a sense *The Old Man and the Sea* is a mini-epic; it is the very smallness of the scale that conveys the atmosphere of vastness. And the two sides of the epic, the private and the cosmic, are now satisfactorily linked in a character. At the same time the very success of the work draws attention to Hemingway's limitations – for, like all his achievements, it is a success by subtraction (just as all his failures are failures of omission). When he succeeds one has the feeling that everything except *exactly* what he wants to say has been pared away. Thus what he does say has great immediacy. Philip Young puts it well:

> It is a world seen through a crack in a wall by a man who is pinned down by gunfire . . . Hemingway's world is a narrow one, which is real to us in a limited and partial way only, for he has left out of it a great deal of what many people would quite simply call 'life'.

That – even if we feel *The Old Man and the Sea* has a less fevered quality, an element of unfevered emotional generosity – is fundamentally true. And so – although it sounds paradoxical – we may speak of Hemingway's achievement as universality of a limited kind. Also – although it sounds suspiciously like Hemingway himself – he made a difference, he mattered.

THOMAS WOLFE

If Hemingway's novels show strange twists and distortions of his public character, there is an absolutely simple one-to-one ratio between Wolfe's personality and his books. Six foot six inches tall, eater of gigantic meals, Brobdignagian strider about the streets, cosmic stretcher of the working day, Thomas Wolfe is very much like one of the implausible Gants of his first two novels (*Look Homeward Angel* and *Of Time and the River*), a family who live on a crude level of emotional intensity unparalleled except – on a more varied and sophisticated level – in the novels of Dostoievsky or Virginia Woolf.

42

Wolfe's novels are wholly autobiographical, a characteristic that began to pall as their number increased. Yet in many respects the hero of each *Bildungsroman* represents more clearly than does any writer except Fitzgerald the shape of the American hero in relation to his society. In both Wolfe and Fitzgerald the individual's search for his own identity, the craving for his own experience is also a search for the identity of America and an understanding of the – or rather *a* – specifically American mode of experience. The difference between them – talent apart – is one of social background; Wolfe's small-town origins, his revolt against the standards and behaviour of the American *petit bourgeois*, coupled with the sense that somehow this same background was important and valuable, is surely typical. It is a situation that other popular writers were to exploit, and the evidence of their success – of the material success of, say, James Michener and Tennessee Williams – is evidence of Wolfe's typicality.

One of the most common criticisms made against the 'social' novel in America, from Twain onwards, is of inconsistency or self-contradiction. Twain, Upton Sinclair, Willa Cather, Sinclair Lewis, Sherwood Anderson all criticise American life and see it as, in many respects, crippling. Yet they manage not only to give an affirmative side to it but to exalt the same qualities that they portray as repressive. In Lewis's work, for example, the very breezy optimism that makes *Babbitt*'s Zenith and the Gopher Prairie of *Main Street* into such hell-holes is offered as an ongoing moral possibility and in some ways a solution to his characters' problems. Some readers have recognised this as a sort of inverted realism – reality is so intolerable that the only *realistic way* of coping is to pretend that it is not like that.

This objection is, I think, naïve and indeed inaccurate, for it misrepresents the nature of America and its varieties of experience. Naturally there are some writers for whom the 'positive' amounts to self-deception. Yet in a writer like Wolfe we can see a very natural and typically American reaction to what is, as a matter of simple fact, a conflict of evidence. Eugene Gant, the hero of *Look Homeward Angel*, sees and experiences intensely both the good and the bad sides of middle-American life. His family is in a sense one long casualty list. His father is a self-pitying libertine who bleeds his children emotionally; his mother is a miser who crams the house with boarders and virtually starves her children; sister Eliza is mad; brother Ben, a sardonic species of American nihilist, dies of tuberculosis; brother Luke turns into a disturbed and demented protocapitalist, and brother Stevie is a worm in every imaginable way. Eugene is torn apart by the conflict of it all.

But – and this is the first sign of a conflict in evidence – he escapes, and the escape works. This is in itself an interesting and positive statement on the nature of America. It is helpful to compare Eugene's experience with that of other middle-class escapees in another time and place. In the nineteenth-century French novel which deals with similar concerns the escaping bourgeois carries his curse with him, if he is able to leave at all. Thus Frederick Moreau of *L'Éducation Sentimentale* and Julien Sorel of *Le Rouge et le Noir* are both destroyed by the same bourgeois values they are escaping from. Eugene simply finds a lot of nice bourgeois who are nice to him. America is presented as a big country, a country large enough for the individual to escape into it.

Secondly, Wolfe sees experience as in itself meaningful. Even when Eugene is suffering we are meant to feel that the very experience is worthwhile. The death of Ben is a good example, for if anything in *Look Homeward Angel* ought to be tragic it is this. Ben is one of Wolfe's best characters, and it would be possible to read into his intelligence, his sarcasm and his bitterness an indictment of the life of grinding routine imposed upon him by his parents. Notice, however, what it is that Wolfe chooses to stress. First Ben's death is described in exultantly dramatic terms:

> Filled with a terrible vision of all life in the one moment, he seemed to rise forward bodilessly from his pillows without support – a flame, a light, a glory – joined at length in death to the dark

spirit who had brooded upon each footstep of his lonely adventure on earth.

Secondly, some explicit instructions are given:

> We can believe in the nothingness of life, we can believe in the nothingness of death and of life after death – but who can believe in the nothingness of Ben?

In other words, *being* Ben, experiencing life as Ben does, is itself a positive, a meaningful thing, no matter what else is true.

An argument of this kind should not lead us into a false estimation of Wolfe's actual achievements, which are extremely limited. Even after the assiduous editing by Maxwell Perkins of the original manuscripts, the books are still much too long, repetitive and not at all well organised. The pervading tone of the works, deriving as it does from emotional extremity, can become monotonous. The whole often seems like Kabuki theatre minus the conventions but with added howls. And, as Thomas Moser pointed out, there is no growth in the main figure, and very little relation between, or impact of events upon, character.

Given these faults, it is interesting to find – and this is much quoted in Wolfe's favour – that Faulkner considered him the best of his contemporaries:

> . . . he tried his best to get it all said; he was willing to throw away style, coherence, all the rules of preciseness, to try to put all the experience of the human heart on the head of a pin, as it were.

The judgement reflects interestingly on Faulkner – who can also be accused of writing to an excessive length – but as a defence it is not very successful. One could easily object that Wolfe could not have 'thrown away' coherence or rules of preciseness since he shows no evidence of ever having known what they were. Also he certainly did not 'throw away style'; indeed, one of the problems of *Look Homeward Angel* consists in its mixture of styles, and particularly in Wolfe's awkward and at times near-illiterate attachment to purple passages full of derivatively gimcrack imagery.

> Like Apollo, who did his penance to the high god in the sad house of King Admetus, he came, a god with broken feet, into the grey hovel of this world . . . O Artemidorus farewell.

Thus Wolfe chooses to ruin his description of Ben's death. 'He tried to get it all said' is most often offered in Wolfe's defence, and there is certainly something in this. One does feel that inside his bad, fat books good, thin ones are fighting to get out. At the same time one must challenge how much was the 'all' that he tried to get said. Wolfe felt, particularly with regard to people, that if one included in a novel everything one knew 'the world' must be in there somewhere. The problem was that Wolfe's 'everything' was limited to his own somewhat limited perceptions. Equally, it is impossible to conceive of understanding without some degree of selection – and selection was foreign to Wolfe.

Still, in one respect Wolfe has made a remarkable development in bringing together twin nightmares – the repressiveness of the small town and the psychotic horrors of the family. These themes were implicitly linked in nineteenth-century American literature – *Huckleberry Finn* is the great example – but they do not collide with such public force until this century. Hemingway deliberately avoids the family; in *For Whom the Bell Tolls*, he refers significantly to Robert Jordan's father's suicide yet deliberately refuses to go into details, to explore the cause of this most primal wound. Similarly, although Fitzgerald's characters are all wounded by family as well as society, it is society that gets the real blame. While this applies conspicuously to all Fitzgerald's novels (in *The Beautiful and Damned*, for example, the possibility of dramatic scenes with Anthony's potentially dramatic grandfather are continually avoided), it is most striking in *Tender is the Night* where, although Nicole's incest with her father has driven her mad, the blame falls not on the family *per se* but on the family as a representative of a certain malignant social type. It may be that neither Fitzgerald nor Hemingway could afford emotionally to really look at families; it is therefore interesting that the subject should receive greater attention in their last books. Hemingway's guilt about his marriage clearly leads to much greater consideration of wife and children in his posthumous *A Moveable Feast* and *Islands in the Stream*. And it is clear from the elaborate plan of *The Last Tycoon* left by Fitzgerald that he intended to develop the question of family relationships already suggested in the narrator's feelings about her father. In a country which worships the notion of familyhood to such an extent, it is remarkable that we should have had to wait so long for its exposition as a great theme. For this exposition – and its mad, sticky flowering in Faulkner – we must give appropriate thanks to Wolfe.

JOHN DOS PASSOS

In Dos Passos we encounter an interesting parallel with Russian literature, for America calls forth the consciousness of geographic size which the Russian novel is never without. Even a drawing-room conversation in Turgenev is carried on in the characters' and the reader's knowledge that outside the building Russia is stretching interminably away. Often in American literature, most obviously in the case of Dos Passos, we find the author trying to come to terms with the sheer size of America, to produce a scale model in words.

Although Dos Passos had previously written several books – notably *Three Soldiers* and *Manhattan Transfer* – it is by his great trilogy, *USA*, that he is most frequently remembered. For all its shortcomings, this is one of the most underrated works in all American literature, and as a consequence there is some strange disproportion in a state of affairs where Dos Passos receives one-tenth of the attention given to Faulkner or Hemingway. Of course, the social content of *USA* is no longer of pressing interest, and Dos Passos is often said to be most interesting as a technician. Then why is there so little discussion of his technique? If his ideas are no longer fashionable, we might at least pay attention to his talent.

The three parts of *USA* are *The 42nd Parallel* (1930) *1919* (1932) and *The Big Money* (1936); together these contain hundreds of characters but focus on a dozen whom we see – some more systematically than others – moving from the pre-war period to the Wall Street crash. As if this span were not wide enough, Dos Passos uses various techniques which increase and intensify the scope. The passages dealing with the characters' lives – which are themselves varied, some presented in an authorially controlled chronicle, some as an edited version of the characters' own thoughts – are interspersed with 'camera eye' and newsreel sections, and biographical sections.

Although this method is often praised, the full magnitude of Dos Passos' success in using it is not sufficiently recognised. Let us take an example from *The 42nd Parallel* – that of the section begun by Newsreel 19. It is difficult to do credit to Dos Passos' newsreels by quotation because a good part of the effect depends upon the cumulative impression of typography and content, creating out of the newsreel something infinitely more poetic and suggestive than one would expect from such 'factual' material. Thus we have headlines:

US AT WAR
UPHOLD NATION CITY'S CRY

followed by the refrain of *the* popular American war song: 'Over there, over there'. We then cut into the middle of a bit of non-headline newspaper reporting:

> ... at the annual meeting of the Colt Patent Firearms Manufacturing Company a $2,500,000 melon was cut. The present capital stock was increased. The profits for the year were 259 per cent.

At this stage we notice the clarity of the impression that is building up; we are dealing with two factors – popular chauvinism and the war as a financial undertaking. The vulgarity of these two ideas is made more bitter by the plaintive quality of the song which, like so many naïvely rousing war songs, is in retrospect almost desperately sad. The next six lines of the newsreel are:

JOYFUL SURPRISE OF BRITISH
'The Yanks are coming
We're coming o-o-o-ver
PLAN LEGISLATION TO KEEP COLORED
PEOPLE FROM WHITE AREAS

These obviously continue the impression made by the earlier lines, while possessing the features that guard against repetitiveness. The impression of naïveté latent in the first section quoted becomes pronounced in that headline about the British – not because it is untrue but because it attributes a spirit of jolly American small-town optimism to a situation that does not warrant it. Secondly, anyone who knows the song recognises – in the protraction of 'over' – that we are coming to its climax. But here Dos Passos withdraws and gives us instead bald new information – information about Negroes that we are hearing for the first time and information presented with the literal matter-of-factness that is the other side of the guilt coin. In other words, if you feel guilty you may adopt a number of tones to cover up – one of them is that of quiet normality. Just as it is normal to be jolly about wars, so – in a different tone, of course – it is normal to legislate against Negroes.

Although the ironies are increasing apace, all of this is still very clear; we know what is being dealt with. What Dos Passos does next is therefore particularly interesting:

many millions paid for golf about Chicago Hindu agitators in nationwide scare Armour urges U.S. save earth from famine.

Now clearly he is running parts of several different newspaper reports together, but as if that were not striking enough he removes all punctuation so that it is difficult to tell where one fragmentary statement ends and another begins. The impression created then is one of rush and of confusion – both of which points characterise the attitude to the war and indeed the state of America itself. (Parenthetically it is worth noticing that Dos Passos has caught two contrary but equally significant emotional attitudes which foreigners continually find in the US. One is that of headlong rush – the desire to get, spend, live faster. The other factor is the linguistic laboriousness with which Americans choose to discuss what is most important to them. One can sense the discussion of the annual meeting of stockholders or the spread of golf ballooning outwards.) It is a sign of extreme artistic care that the moment of stylistic confusion should also be the moment of maximum irony. For the original ironies we noticed are being built into something more – a criticism of American unreflectiveness, smugness and parochialism. The millions paid for golf are of the same importance as the fate of the sub-continent of India; the firm urging the US to save the world from famine is a meat firm, seeking under a philanthropic mask the increase in its own production (and notice – a neat bit of selection this – that the meat company is called Armour, particularly appropriate in time of war).

We need not go farther with the analysis of this newsreel; it is plainly a poignant evocation of the *tone* of American smugness, and it certainly shows that, in these most 'factual' parts of *USA*, Dos Passos was behaving like an artist. He does not simply stick together convenient sections of contemporary material; he selects very carefully, and he shapes, alters, contracts and arranges it in a way that evokes many parallels in modern art.

The newsreel is succeeded by a 'camera eye' section which describes a sea crossing to France followed by a description of France itself. Generally speaking these sections represent the author's own impressions and experiences, although the way in which the stream of consciousness used detaches itself from any specific 'I' and provides a counterpoint to the material contained in the other sections lessens so specific an effect, and merges into the whole. This particular section, 'Camera Eye (27)', evokes place and does so beautifully. It also contains some pointed ironic observation. There is a very neat (and quasi-Hemingwayan) repetition of 'brave' – so that one can hear the people congratulating themselves on their bogus courage.

> ... anyhow everybody was very brave except for Colonel and Mrs. Knowlton of the American Red Cross who had waterproof coldproof submarineproof suits like Eskimo-suits and they wore them and they sat up on deck with the suits all blown up and only their faces showing and there were first-aid kits in the pockets and in the belt there was a waterproof container with milk-chocolate and crackers and malted-milk tablets.
>
> and in the morning you'd walk round the deck and there would be Mr. Knowlton blowing up Mrs. Knowlton
> or Mrs. Knowlton blowing up Mr. Knowlton.
> the Roosevelt boys were very brave in stiff-visored new American army caps and sharpshooter medals on the khaki whipcord and they talked all day about We must come in We must come in
> as if the war were a swimming pool.

A passage like that surely gives the lie to Seymour Smith's view that 'his creative imagination was deficient'. Indeed what we have in Dos Passos is not merely the variety within each section but variety between the sections.

Here the 'camera eye' is followed by a biographical section – in this case, La Follette, one of his political heroes – the style of which, while distinct, is a subtle combination of the styles of the newsreel and 'camera eye' in its mixture of factual and poetical:

> and he died
> an orator haranguing from the capitol of a lost republic;
> but we will remember
> how he sat firm in March nineteen seventeen while Woodrow Wilson was being inaugurated for the second time, and for three

days held the vast machine at deadlock. They wouldn't let him
speak; the galleries glared hate at him; the Senate was a lynching
party.
    a stumpy man with a lined face, one leg stuck out in the aisle and
his arms folded and a chewed cigar in the corner of his mouth
    and an undelivered speech on his desk
    a wilful man expressing no opinion but his own.

I doubt whether anyone else using the novel form has been able
so immediately to convey the poetry of the smallest factual de
tails or to show the intensely poetic possibility of the most con
ventionally unpoetic things. The technical achievement of the
work as a whole seems more considerable when we recognise the
book's size; the overall success of Dos Passos' 'poeticism' is
extraordinary. By comparison with other novelists – such as John
Updike – who have used 'poetic' intentions, he shines.

Of course, style is not everything, and there are a number of
other technical points in Dos Passos' favour. His dialogue is
superbly realistic. The merchant sailor Joe Williams, the social
climber Eleanor Stoddard, the young Irishman Mac – all speak
and think with complete and convincing distinctiveness. More
than that, Dos Passos manages alterations in his characters and
their communication; this is a comparatively rare achievement in
a novelist – Tolstoy is usually held up as one of its few exponents.
J. Ward Moorhouse and Eveline Hutchins are two of the main
characters who change as the trilogy goes on. Moorhouse (some
times wrongly described as the book's central character – nothing
is central in *USA* except the country itself) moves from being the
sort of hick who can write:

Dear Annabelle,
    I now realize that you have intended all along to use me only as a
    screen for your disgraceful and unwomanly conduct. I now under-
    stand why you prefer the company of foreigners, bohemians and
    such to that of ambitious young Americans.

to a smooth-grained public relations man who would never commit himself to anything so provincial. And Eveline – one of his more interesting portrayals who, in a different novel, would be a tragic figure – moves (like a James heroine gone wrong) from fresh enthusiasm for life through a series of unsatisfactory sexual affairs to suicide.

The characterisation of *USA* is frequently criticised. Not all the main characters have the same imaginative reality as those I have cited, but remarkably few are flat and none is incredible. If one considers both the distinctness and variety of major and minor figures (many of whom have a positively Dickensian vividness) one cannot argue that they are simply types. They are typical – but that is a different thing.

For Dos Passos' intention, as the title of the trilogy suggests, was to produce an intelligently typical picture of the United States – a picture which was therefore both panorama and portrait, indeed a panorama that depended upon a whole series of portraits. In this, Dos Passos confirms Carlyle's view that history is the essence of innumerable biographies; what he wants to show us is how the specific essences flow into the one great essence. Specifically, he was interested in the life of the whole, and how individuals are affected by it. So pronounced is this feature of Dos Passos' work that it has sometimes been argued that he 'belongs' with certain Marxist or neo-Marxist writers of the early twentieth century. In *USA* several of the characters embrace Marxism only to find it has been corrupted by *apparatchiks* and party bosses. However, it is not clear at this stage whether or not he believed it was a noble idea which, given an improvement in human nature, would be the answer; later on, he turned into a kind of patriotic conservative – a switch that many of his critics find unconvincing. It has also been suggested (he read French and knew French literature) that he was influenced by the French disciple of unanism, Jules Romains. This is not impossible, for Romains' unanism holds that collective emotions – particularly those of groups – are in some senses superior to individual ones. However, unanism is itself merely a reflection of the generally increased awareness of the relationship between the individual and the group – an awareness which came to fascinate and stayed to haunt the twentieth century.

In American literature its manifestation is particularly poignant – after all, the country prided itself on a combination of individual freedom and group solidarity. Certainly Dos Passos had no time for groups which did not allow individual freedom. In one of his earliest travel books, *Rosinante to the Road Again*, he praises the Spanish communes because their group solidarity still involves a 'strong anarchistic reliance on the individual man' and the conviction that 'only the individual soul is real'. It is possible to see in Dos Passos' subordination of character to the overall structure, a fear of the power of structures and an essentially pessimistic future for the individual in their grip. The point is certainly borne out by the fact that Dos Passos' characters come to at best unhappy and at the worst disastrous ends, and that their fate does appear to be society's fault.

The point is emphasised by his treatment of actual historical figures. Those whom he likes – La Follette, Thorstein Veblen, Frank Lloyd Wright – are all individualists who suffer at the hands of society, while his historical villains – Andrew Carnegie, Henry Ford, Pierpont Morgan – are all systems men. In some unpleasant inversion of unanism, each created a system which outgrew those who controlled it; the system came to have a life of its own and to crush the life of the individuals involved with it. Dos Passos carefully stresses how, in each case, the system has turned out to be a Frankenstein's monster to its progenitor. At the end of 'Tin Lizzie', his section on Henry Ford, we see Ford living 'besieged on his father's farm' and having 'the new highway where the new model cars roared and slithered and hissed oilily' moved

> so that everything might be
> the way it used to be,
> in the days of horses and buggies.

Here Dos Passos shows himself as a large and powerful link in a historical chain. What J. C. Furnas calls the 'manipulative origin' of many great American fortunes had grown speedily more apparent from 1850 onwards. (Looking back to Nick's job in *Gatsby* it is interesting to notice how many of those fortunes hinged on the bond business.) The concern of Congress with anti-trust legislation was in itself a barometric reading of the extent to which money-systems were running away from individual control; and close examination of the workings of trusts shows how far millionaires themselves were removed from contact with the actual source of their money. It is, of course, exactly that problem, multiplied a million times on a millionth of the scale, that ran riot in the Wall Street crash of 1929, when every bus driver had a broker and the market was white hot with imaginary money. This fear of the system, of which anti-trust sentiment is merely one part, is with us still. Kurt Vonnegut's *God Bless You Mr Rosewater* attacks – in a peculiar and funny way – the monstrous impersonality of a financial trust, while each of Norman Mailer's 'journalistic' works shows the fear that America has become a 'corporation' (the conduct of the Vietnam war did a lot to increase that fear). Dos Passos, therefore, stands in a direct line of tradition; he must be given credit for expressing it so articulately in literary terms. Others had noticed it before him – Upton Sinclair and Dreiser spring to mind – but they treat it only by implication; their concern is on a more immediately personal level (as was Dickens'). Dos Passos was the first writer to isolate and charge with passion a concern which was growing the world over, as Huxley and Orwell testify.

Yet the word 'isolate' creates the wrong impression, for it is in the sheer volume of observations of American society that so much of Dos Passos' reputation consists. Each of the observations is fragmented into the behaviour of the characters and then re-assembled in newsreel/'camera eye'/biographical sections. There is, for example, the question of upward social mobility. Most of

Dos Passos' characters are on the make socially even more than financially; they are in pursuit of a weird and ill-defined gentility which seems to have as one of its few characterising features a sense of aloofness, of separation from the manners of the great mass. It is the very vagueness – by comparison with Europe – of this snobbery that makes it self-defeating. For, although it could be said that all snobbery is ultimately unsatisfying, the presence of stricter codes and more obvious barriers makes the activity of the English social climber more complex, so that he is likely to become frustrated by the sheer continuing magnitude of the task. The English snob gets tired climbing, while the American snob (unless he goes to England) may find that the arrival has no substance, shape or meaning; his frustration is therefore of a different kind and Dos Passos captures it well; his characters start frantically spiralling upwards only to find that there is nowhere for them to go. At the same time he makes us understand why the spiralling should take place at all, because the characters who want merely to live – that is, to treat life as if it were a source of non-competitive satisfaction (like Joe Williams the seaman or Mac the union man) – are destroyed by society; destroyed not for sitting still, for then they would be cogs in the machine, but for determinedly refusing to go upwards on the spiral.

Dos Passos notices, too, and hammers away at the fact, that the war is an economic swindle, that all wars are an economic swindle. He was one of the first novelists to notice this and among the most forceful in pointing it out. War is simply another form of the general exploitation made possible, in part at least, by America's own peculiar home-grown brand of self-deception – which, again, Dos Passos observes beautifully.

The biographical section on Teddy Roosevelt is a good example. 'Righteousness', says Dos Passos, 'was his by birth.' Everything for Teddy was 'bully': big-game hunting, trust-busting, fighting gimmicky wars with gimmicky volunteer armies but with ungimmicky results:

. . . it wasn't bully huddling under puptents in the tropical rain or scorching in the morning sun of the seared Cuban hills with malaria mowing them down and dysentery and always yellowjack to be afraid of.

In fact the world is not bully, although great sections of the United States – Teddy included – are encouraged to believe it is. In *A Room With a View* E. M. Forster says that the greatest division in the world exists between those who do and those who do not live by catchwords. The danger of those who do is an especially American problem. It is the danger that Sinclair Lewis outlined in *Babbitt* and *Main Street*, and that Dos Passos sees not only in Teddy – 'his pet phrases: Strenuous Life, Realizable Ideals, Just Government' – but in so many of the characters of *USA*. In America the point has particular relevance since the country sees itself in such idealistic terms. The point is universally recognised, but anyone who doubts it need only open a non-national American newspaper or tune in to a local American radio station and he will find in half an hour's reading or listening more declaration of ideals, and more taking of ideals for granted, than he would meet in England in a year.

Out of the great run of Dos Passos' social observation, let us take one more example: his treatment of the relationship between the land and industry, on which he takes a stand very far removed from that of facile romanticism, and distinct also from some of the attitudes prevalent in earlier American fiction. One of the oddities of literary history is that so many authors – Hawthorne, Thoreau, Cather, Anderson – condemned the hypocrisy, smugness and general repressiveness of small, predominantly rural communities without linking the causes of their behaviour to the land. Indeed, the land continues for some time to possess the healing properties traditionally designated for it in Romantic literature. In the woods Thoreau can again recover his sense of individuality. As industrialism increases, the contrast becomes more pointed; and it is not surprising that, in a country with so much countryside, the possibility of escape should still exist. Thus, although rural communities may be condemned, the countryside itself escapes blame – at worst it is displayed as frightening, as in Twain or Melville or even Sinclair Lewis, but the fear has a splendour and a grandeur to it. This attitude is not altogether realistic. Nature can destroy as well as heal; and, historically speaking, men who have left the land for city life have not universally done so at their spiritual peril or for trivial reasons. The town may heal what the country has destroyed and vice versa; it all depends on the individual.

It is typically straight-sighted of Dos Passos to recognise this. Many of the characters of *USA* escape from the intolerable drudgery of farm life to the city and industry. Of his historical figures, Bill Haywood, the union leader, was 'bound . . . out to a farmer, he ran away because the farmer lashed him with a whip'; Henry Ford leaves his father's farm to get a job in a Detroit machine shop; Thorstein Veblen 'hated the irk of ever-repeated backbreaking chores round the farm', and for ever after his periodic returns to the country are far from life-giving, he retreats bitterly into it like a defeated man. It is not surprising, therefore, that there is a complete absence of pastoral sacramentalism in *USA*. The characters do not lift their eyes to the hills whence might come their aid.

There is no doubt that overall *USA* represents a considerable achievement. But, ultimately, the book fails to reach the highest epic standards. Size does not necessarily correspond to scope, and length need not bring depth. Dos Passos' historical-philosophic points are hermetically sealed in the newsreel and biographical sections; they do not inter-relate with the individual lives he portrays elsewhere.

Another major drawback is the effect of his moral sense; it appears dissociated and externalised. The implication in every one of the social catastrophes he observes is of the existence of a very simple set of 'shalls' and 'shall nots' which apparently come from man's own inner knowledge. Yet, judging by the speed with which his characters abandon or fail to find satisfaction from such a morality, one wonders how much he really believed in it – a typically twentieth-century American dilemma.

There can be no doubt, however, that Dos Passos is a novelist of considerable importance and, from a historical as well as a literary standpoint, of great interest.

JOHN STEINBECK

If Dos Passos has not received the full measure of credit for his achievement, how much more critical hostility has John Steinbeck had to face. When awarded the 1962 Nobel Prize for Literature, he was promptly booed. The reaction was not merely from the disgruntled supporters of Robert Frost but represented the strong feeling that a disastrous mistake had been made. From very early days even enthusiastic critics had found it hard to accept Steinbeck's eclectic production. How could the man who wrote *The Grapes of Wrath* also write something as trivial and mushy as *Sweet Thursday*? (Hemingway, encountering a piece of Steinbeck's wartime film propaganda, *Bombs Away*, said he would rather cut three fingers off his throwing hand than write something like it.) Critics who dislike Steinbeck simply find the same things wrong with all his books and are only prepared to grant even *The Grapes of Wrath* either a modest niche in the museum of 'modern American realism', or a still smaller place in the 'game, sincere but ill-educatedly pretentious' section, into which much worthless junk is thrown.

Steinbeck's work ranges from *Cup of Gold, A Life of Sir Henry Morgan, Buccaneer with Occasional References to History* (an historical romance with heavy debts to the grail quest myth) through strange semi-comic pastoral vignettes (*Of Mice and Men* and *Cannery Row*) to the 'conventional but awkwardly symbolic' *East of Eden, Winter of Our Discontent*. This varied output is a tribute to the cheerful and typically American enthusiasm for alighting sportingly on different subjects (itself perhaps a product of American education), but it is *The Grapes of Wrath* which constitutes his claim to major literary achievement. I find it hard to accept the strictures which would keep it from its rightful place as an essentially *American* American novel, of great power.

The Grapes of Wrath deals of course with the social situation caused by the Oklahoma Dust Bowl disaster of the 1930s. This Steinbeck describes at the opening of the novel – drought comes, destroying the corn and cotton, drying out the topsoil, then gales scatter whole fogs of dust across the countryside.

> The dawn came, but no day. In the grey sky a red sun appeared, a dim ⸱⁺ˡe circle that gave a little light, like dusk; and as that day advanced, the dusk slipped back towards darkness, and the wind cried and whimpered over the fallen corn … When the night came again it was black night, for the stars could not pierce the dust to get down, and the window lights could not even spread beyond their own yards. Now the dust was evenly mixed with the air, an emulsion of dust and air.

Those sections read like the description of a plague; the coming of a great natural disaster that appals by its very unnaturalness. The normal processes of nature – sun, moon, day, night – are inverted and blurred into one monochromatic nightmare. A very similar process is enacted by the landlords, banks and financial organisations which hold the mortgages for the land; farmhouses, fences, boundaries are obliterated until one great uniform mass is produced – produced, note, by another such mass, the non-human, non-distinguishing monolithic corporation: 'The man sitting in the iron seat did not look like a man: gloved, goggled, rubber dust-mask over nose and mouth, he was a part of the monster, a robot in the seat. And this monster is caused by another:

> If a bank or a finance company owned the land, the owner man said: The Bank – or the Company – needs – wants – insists – must

have – as though the Bank or the Company were a monster, with thought and feeling, which had ensnared them. These last would take no responsibility for the banks or the companies because they were men and slaves, while the banks were machines and masters all at the same time.

Steinbeck must be given credit for the intelligence with which he views the question, refusing to take refuge either in the absurdly optimistic belief that the individual can cope with everything or that the machine is a completely powerful entity utterly removed from individual control. One of the most sensibly realistic things about the book is his establishing early on that corporations are groups of individuals gone wrong, and it is this fact that gives some philosophic meaning to his continual positive statements – as, for example:

> 'I got to figure,' the tenant said. 'We all got to figure. There's some way to stop this. It's not like lightning or earthquakes. We've got a bad thing made by men, and by God that's something we can change.'

If the machine were not run by individuals, the corporation not manned by them, that statement would be a lot of folksy baloney, and the Joads' journey merely masochistic. Driven from their farm by drought and foreclosures, the entire family load themselves into the modern equivalent of a covered wagon and, charmed by stories of prosperity and possibility, head West for California. To say that their journey is epic is rather like saying that the *Iliad* has a strong story line. Each forward move represents victory over what ought to be unbearable odds, each slip backwards is bitterly contested. Through death and desertion the Joads keep their humanity and generosity. It is the story not only of physical and material but also of spiritual struggle. However much readers may dispute the philosophic use Steinbeck makes of the Joads, there can be no doubt that the details of their lives and the whole social fabric are superbly and convincingly accurate. And no wonder – not only did Steinbeck report for the *San*

Francisco News on the plight of migratory labourers, he also shared their experiences, working alongside them, travelling with them from Oklahoma to California and staying in their labour camps.

A testament to the accuracy of his portrayal was the enormous defensive reaction roused by the novel. The county agent for Sequoyah County, Oklahoma – the setting of the novel's early scenes – protested that his area was not a dust-bowl and did not have many tractors; while another man stated in the name of himself and his dad and mother, whose hair was silvery in the service of America, that Steinbeck had produced 'a black, infernal creation of a twisted, distorted mind'. But, when *The Grapes of Wrath* was made into a film, Darryl Zanuck sent private investigators to test conditions amongst the Okies; they reported that things were even worse than Steinbeck had suggested. *Life* magazine – perhaps distrusting Zanuck's capacity for disinterested observation – produced photographs that told the same story. Indeed the grape boycott of the 1960s, through which Cesar Chavez finally succeeded in forming a union for Californian agricultural workers, attracted publicity which, if it did not show social conditions as bad as Steinbeck's, certainly revealed an appallingly high incidence of extreme poverty and disease among migrant workers – and this in a boom economy. So, although Steinbeck may be accused of sentimentalising people's reactions to the conditions, he did portray accurately the conditions themselves.

But, of course, literal accuracy is worth only so much; in Steinbeck's case it has the force of extreme passion rooted in dramatic scenes. It is, as Henry Steele Commager says, 'a tract for the times, a campaign document', in the sense that Steinbeck desperately wants us to change things – but his method is rooted in our caring for the people and caring what happens to them. It is in this area that Steinbeck's critics divide; no one disputes the dramatic force of what happens to the Joads, or the continuing

sense of tension and struggle that combating the events entails –
indeed, the nearest thing to a protest comes to the grotesqueness
of Ma, lying all night next to Granma's corpse, not telling anyone
of the death because '. . . we couldn' he'p her. The fambly had ta
get acrost. I tol' her, tol' her when she was a-dyin. We couldn'
stop in the desert. There was the young ones – an Rosasharn's
baby. I tol' her.' That, however, is Ma's reaction after the event.
Steinbeck never describes in detail or dwells on the events of that
night, thus uniting our impression with Ma's – that it is a terrible
thing, but one which must be borne, and fuss will not help the
enduring.

A more substantial objection – from Harry T. Moore – is that
certain of the scenes (the disappearance of Rosasharn's husband,
Connie Rivers; the falling off of Noah Joad, the eldest and simple-
minded son who finds a river and, unable to endure leaving it,
abandons the family; and the storm which drives them from their
box-car camp to a barn where Rosasharn can be brought into
contact with a starving man for the novel's amazing end) are
either inconsequential or 'placed' for effect. It is not the scene
per se which is objected to so much as the use to which it is put,
particularly in relation to character. The scene, it is said, is planted
to indulge the characters and their views of life – a process which
may come dangerously close to robbing the characters of their
reality.

I do not myself agree with the charge. Noah has from the beginning been convincingly portrayed as simple-minded, and the
disappearance of Connie strikes me as very realistic. In the law
courts a great many cases of desertion concern one partner in a
marriage who, without any explicit warning, simply walks out
rather than stay and face his guilt, and such behaviour is exactly
consonant with Connie's silliness and general weakness. The
storm scene, too, is well-prepared for, the rains having been
forecast for some time.

The book is also accused of sentimentality. Critics, such as

Edmund Wilson, who disliked the novel, find this particularly evident in the characters' positivism; again and again they express their indomitability, their belief in the essential possibility of life in terms verging on the idiotic. This is a typical conversation between Pa and Ma Joad:

> 'An kin we feed a extra mouth . . . Kin we, Ma?'
> Ma cleared her throat. 'It ain't kin we? It's will we?' she said firmly. 'As far as "Kin", we can't do nothin'; but as far as "will", why we'll do what we will. An as far as "will" – it's a long time our folks been here . . . an I never heard tell of no Joads . . . ever refusin' food an' shelter or a lift on the road to anybody that asked. They's been mean Joads, but never that mean.'

For some this is *faux-naïf*, stagy and philosophically obtrusive; under a pretence of natural speech the characters' – and Steinbeck's – philosophy is being rammed unnaturally down our throats. Indeed the dialogue is reminiscent of the kind of excess mocked at by Nabokov in his afterword to *Lolita*:

> . . . one reader suggested that his firm might consider publication [of *Lolita*] if I turned Lolita into a twelve-year-old lad and had him seduced by Humbert, a farmer, in a barn, amidst gaunt and arid surroundings, all this set forth in short, strong, 'realistic' sentences ('He acts crazy. We all act crazy, I guess. I guess God acts crazy.' Etc).

This sort of thing was certainly prevalent in Steinbeck's time; it was a quality of Anderson's satirised by Hemingway in *The Torrents of Spring*, and the curious reader who is fond of literary aspidistras might seek it out in Erskine Caldwell's *God's Little Acre*. Yet, although Steinbeck is not entirely innocent of this militantly manipulative simplicity, which causes problems, for example, in *Tortilla Flat*, we may absolve him, I think, as far as *The Grapes of Wrath* is concerned. For instance, in that quotation, the distinction Ma makes between 'Kin' and 'will' is an important one. It expresses the difference between the way they feel about life and the way life is; and the difference between everything they have previously lived by – the whole moral justification of American rural life – and the selfish immoral impersonality that is attempting to supplant it. What Ma is doing here is convincing Pa (notice that he wavers – showing that the Joads are very far from being the 100-per-cent angels which adverse critics would have us believe) that morality is morality no matter how circumstances change. It is also practical advice – the one hope the Joads of this world have is that by sticking together and to their principles they will overcome. We see this working repeatedly in the book, as in the scene where a woman in a café sells them food cheaply, not out of pity but from a sense of common humanity.

The problem of how to portray the speech, thought patterns and beliefs of 'simple people' is one of historic proportions; as William Empson has shown, the whole notion of 'pastoral' as a form involves an, at times, uneasy relationship between the simple and the sophisticated. Pastoral is a form intended to convey profound simplicity to complex people. Thus, in a sense, there is always a degree of manipulation about it. As many readers will know, one of the central difficulties that emerges from Wordsworth's *Preface to the Lyrical Ballads* is how to use 'naturally' a form of language that needs editing – that is, how to give the *impression* of simplicity of language combined with profundity of feeling without lapsing one way into crudity or the other way into manipulation. The question is one of balance – not an easy quality to achieve, and lapses on the part of, writers who attempt it are traditionally pardoned. We may ask, therefore, why so little latitude is granted to Steinbeck.

The answer lies in our implicit expectations about pastoral. We extend some measure of toleration towards a sophisticated man struggling to use and show simplicity; we are less happy with a simple man trying to do the same. This is precisely what Steinbeck is, and does. He is a simple man holding to simple philosophic notions, which he allows simple people to produce *exactly as they do in life.* This last part is important; Steinbeck is often accused of allowing his characters too much philosophic reflection, making their dialogue too deliberately pregnant with meaning. Yet, if you listen to an American dirt-farmer, that is very much how he talks. There is in the American rural temperament a limitless capacity for vocal philosophising – philosophising of a particularly Joad-like character, yoking the practical to the metaphysical.

Against this we could argue that while this may be life it is not art; however life-like his material, Steinbeck should shape it better. The charge could only be refuted by lengthy argument; here I can merely make the point that the various elements of *The Grapes of Wrath* suffer from being treated out of context. The language is used in a more intelligent way than is often believed (Granpa and the Dostoievskian Uncle John sometimes utter deep thoughts but they are frequently funny and occasionally ridiculous) and it operates differently in context. Dr Johnson pointed out that hanging concentrates a man's mind wonderfully, and there is no better justification for speculations on the meaning of life than the repeated disasters that occur throughout *The Grapes of Wrath.*

There remains one important criticism of the book: it is hardly convincing to point out that Steinbeck is offering us 'the American motif: a celebrational sense of life', bringing with it a feeling of spiritual optimism, when facts are so horribly and conclusively against the Joads. As F. W. Watt indicates, most of Steinbeck's sympathetic characters – those whom he respects – are social failures: 'they may *survive*, but they do not *succeed*'. The Joads' spiritual optimism is associated with the possibility of a small measure of social and material success – the possibility, at the very least, of not being exploited. Again and again Steinbeck's celebrational sense of life hinges on a belief in the *possibility* of America – it is this which makes the Joads generous – yet at the novel's splendid end, as Rosasharn, her child dead, offers the milk from her breast to the starving man, we can hardly believe that all the spiritual magnificence in the world is going to triumph over the economic facts of the Depression. It seems here as if the specifically American connection between dream and practicality – mentioned earlier – is played out. And it is here that some of Steinbeck's left-wing critics lost patience and accused him of woolly-minded evasion: as in his previous novel, *In Dubious Battle*, Steinbeck should be more radical; he should pay for his social optimism in serious social terms. These same critics find the toying with social explanations in *The Grapes of Wrath* distastefully evasive. Witness the final speech of Tom who, wanted by the police, is finally forced to abandon the family he has fought so hard to keep together.

> Ma said: 'How'm I gonna know bout you? They might kill ya an I wouldn' know. They might hurt ya. How'm I gonna know?'
> Tom laughed uneasily. 'Well, maybe like Casey says, a fella ain't got a soul of his own, but on'y a piece of a big one – an then – . . . Then it don' matter. Then I'll be aroun' in the dark. I'll be ever'-where – wherever you look. Whenever they's a fight so hungry people can eat, I'll be there. Whenever they's a cop beatin' up a guy, I'll be there . . . An when our folks eat the stuff they raise an' live in the houses they build – why I'll be there.'

Spiritual and practical explanations seem to be mixed up there. In exactly what sense will Tom be 'aroun' when there is trouble? Is Steinbeck saying that the people will overcome social obstacles because the force of their collective spirit will be ultimately un-stoppable? Or is he advocating through Tom an actual social programme of guerilla-like unrest? The problem, Steinbeck's opponents would say, is that Tom is only too likely, on account of his Joad-like purity and directness, to be flung immediately into the penitentiary – whence he will be hard put to it to be 'aroun' in any useful way. Of course, this action could be fitted into one side of the Marxist analysis (if Tom is arrested and jailed his example will go marching on), but the practical results of this, given the Okies' capacity for puzzled acquiescence, is all too likely, when confronted by massive institutional force, to be nil. In which case 'the folks' are never going to 'eat the stuff they raise an' live in the houses they build'. There is, then, in Steinbeck a conflict (to quote Martin Seymour-Smith) 'between the philosophic unanimist and the humane socialist' – in other words, a belief in the strength of collective *spirit* is inconsonant with even the moderate social reforms which he, admittedly in very general terms, advocates.

But this is an *American* novel dealing with an *American* reality. Just as dirt farmers do not speak like products of Princeton (nor for that matter *how* products of Princeton believe they should speak), so the American people are not given to massive social protest. One of the points emerging from Dos Passos' work is that, though 'the people's' flag may be deepest red, the *American* people do not care. In short, no matter how great the social provocation offered, there are certain forms of social action which Americans will not take. Yet this observation, greeted as a great truth in Dos Passos, is condemned in Steinbeck. Why? Because Steinbeck is that unfashionable creature, an optimist who believes that things need not stop there, that there may still be a good social result from Depression and disaster.

Yet Steinbeck may well be right. Historians differ, but the United States does show a considerable capacity for non-violent reform; successive state and federal governments *have* responded to pressure from lower down; for the great mass of the people things have, materially speaking at any rate, got better. This is not to say that the United States is perfect – there are still immense problems posed by both urban and rural poverty – it is merely to indicate the tendency towards possible adaptation and improvement. Only history will show whether America in this century becomes increasingly monolithic, inhuman and destructive or, for all its faults, increasingly humane, responsible and decent. Either may happen, but the very existence of the possibility validates the Joads' hopes. It is no use pretending that it is factually true that the course of America is increasingly and irreversibly downwards and that there is no future for people of the Joads' class. Of course, this does not mean that the Joads themselves will survive; it is a hard and terrible fact that they may not. But that too is something Steinbeck has persistently considered – the optimism the Joads display is not for their own future alone (they hope for that although they always know they may go under), but for that of 'the people'. Indeed, the more one becomes conscious of that distinction, the more one realises how much the novel is misunderstood. For the struggle which Steinbeck measures is really one of the oldest American themes: that between spiritual conviction and practical possibility – a struggle that becomes all the more poignant and all the more realistic as it takes place in a country where the two sometimes have, perhaps will and frequently may come together. It is this which makes that conversation between Ma and Tom realistic in observation.

A few social side-issues of the novel are worth raising, partly because they occur in other writers and partly because their very presence testifies to the power of Steinbeck's observation. Indeed, *The Grapes of Wrath* acts as a microcosm for many ideas currently thought of as most tellingly modern. First, the question of landlordism and ownership – the notion that America was suffering and was likely to continue to suffer from landlordism was not new; in the last quarter of the nineteenth century Henry George had outlined the problem in his influential book, *Progress and Poverty* (based on conditions in California) while, in his best-selling novel, *Looking Backward*, Edward Bellamy put the case for public ownership as the answer. In his attitude towards the question of who owns the country and by what right, Steinbeck reveals a very typical American ambivalence, which still persists and sometimes puzzles native Americans as much as outsiders. On the one hand, there is the feeling voiced by one of Steinbeck's characters that 'she's a nice country. But she was stole a long time ago', suggesting the people's right to what the landlords have sequestered. On the other hand, there is the realisation that the people originally pinched the land from the Indians and Mexicans who 'could not resist because they wanted nothing in the world as frantically as the Americans wanted land'. Yet accompanying this is a certain pride in land-grabbing:

> And now the squatting men stood up angrily. Grampa took up the land, and he had to kill the Indians and drive them away. And Pa was born here and he killed weeds and snakes.

There appears to be little moral distinction between snakes and Indians, and one might expect Steinbeck, if not his characters, to equate the two forms of theft: landlords from Okies, Okies from Indians. It is interesting to notice how completely Steinbeck's capacity for moral distinction misses that out. His criticism of California, for instance, is that the passing of the very 'feral hunger, the gnawing, tearing hunger for land' that dispossessed the original natives, brings an accompanying weakening of man's sacramental attitude towards the land: 'they arose in the dark no more to hear the birds' first chattering and the morning wind around the house'. And when 'these things were lost . . . crops were reckoned in dollars . . . until they were no longer farmers at all, but little shop-keepers of crops . . .'. Similarly he turns burning moral attention to those who misuse the sacrament of the land, while telling us that the sacrament was itself based, in part at least, on brutality, violence and theft.

Briefly, a few more social points. Steinbeck, as one critic puts it, has discovered 'the artistic redemption of the machine', for while the tractor that ploughs its way inexorably through houses is seen as ghastly, the Joads' jalopy is seen as a character in itself. Again Steinbeck shows himself as typically American; it is impossible to imagine travelling across twentieth-century America without machinery, or writing one of America's innumerable travel novels without a machine. (*On the Road* would presumably be *By The*

Roadside). One of the more amusing features of recent novels in which characters are bent on rediscovering the beating of a green heart amidst the twisted mechanical wreckage that they see as modern America is that they continually drive around making their discoveries in motor cars. America is never able to turn against machinery in the absolute way of certain English writers (D. H. Lawrence and E. M. Forster are two good examples), nor is it entirely happy with the self-conscious, young mannishly intellectual machine worshipping gone in for by W. H. Auden and Stephen Spender in the 1930s. Like Dos Passos, Steinbeck knows that a machine depends very much on who sees it and what it is used on. Again the spiritual value is yoked to the practical.

Steinbeck also picks up an important social thread when he portrays the increasing foreignness of the native American. The huge European immigration of the last part of the nineteenth century had added a more truly foreign note to American society, whose population had previously been swelled by Scots and Irish – and therefore by principally English-speaking immigrants. American literature quickly begins to reflect the problems of those immigrants who – ignorant of the language and customs, used only to barbarous conditions – can easily be exploited. The most classic cry against their ill-treatment comes in Upton Sinclair's *The Jungle* and Willa Cather's *My Ántonia*, but the twentieth-century novel is still full of the problem. In *The Great Gatsby* one of the most squalid of the dust-choked areas bisected by the West-Egg-to-New-York train is an immigrant one; in *Main Street* the heroine tries her best to make the town treat its Swedish immigrants like people (also in *Gatsby* the Swedes come off badly – in order to collect his Swedish cleaner, Nick makes an almost glancingly described trip into squalor); in Faulkner's *The Sound and the Fury* the poor child who attaches itself to Quentin Compson is the product of Italian immigrants. One of the curious features of each of these books is that the plight of the immigrant – in so far as it is recognised as such – strengthens the sense of

71

displacement already felt by the character who encounters him. In Sinclair Lewis the explanation given is that we are 'all immigrants'; once upon a time every American emigrated from somewhere else – and this may to some extent account for the uneasy feeling of displacement that dogs so much of American life, highlighting the treatment of immigrants who are frequently feared, not only because they are obviously alien in language and behaviour but because they illustrate the flux, the dangerous impermanence of a man's relationship with his own land. In Steinbeck we see the strange American habit of turning everyone who is a nuisance into a non-American. The Okies become virtually a race apart; they have to press their claim:

> We aint foreign. Seven generations back American, and beyond that Irish, Scottish, English, German. One of our folks in the Revolution, an' they was lots of our folks in the Civil War – both sides. Americans.

The Okies become not only non-American but, to borrow a political term, un-American. Casey and Tom, simply because they show some opposition to the intolerable social conditions of the migrant labour camps, are accused of being 'commies'. What we see gradually developing here is to become more pronounced as the century goes on – namely, the dual feelings (both strong) of being an American and not being sure what that means. Nowadays so many characters in American novels travel their native country like foreigners looking for someone or something that will tell them either where home is or how to recognise it if they find it.

CHAPTER 2

The Fate of the Traditional Novel

William Faulkner and John Updike

My consideration of Faulkner and Updike together is not arbitrary. Despite the differences in their generations and background, there are many surprising similarities in their work – one of these is particularly relevant to the future of the American novel: each author produces work which shows the contrary pulls of structure and the absence of structure. By this I do not mean that each writes some books which are structured and some which are not; I mean that repeatedly one encounters in their novels structures adopted and abandoned, and finds therefore one of the great problems of the twentieth-century novel – the relationship between order and meaning on the one hand, and chaos and nonsense on the other, a struggle which is fought out not only through their themes but through the very texture of the works themselves. The consequences for the novel's traditional habit of expressing all its themes (even ones of formlessness) in a formal structure are interesting – as interesting as the future of its traditional techniques.

However, it would be distorting to each of these authors to present his work in terms of one aspect; and, before we can see how that aspect operates, we should take a more detailed look at their work. This is particularly necessary in Faulkner's case since, if one were to take a poll among serious American readers as to who is their most important novelist of this century, his name would, I am sure, comfortably top the list.

WILLIAM FAULKNER

In quantity as well as quality Faulkner appears to outstrip so many of his contemporaries. Even those who see his work in the later part of his career as declining (from *The Unvanquished* onwards) would point to *The Sound and the Fury* as one of the greatest novels not only of the twentieth century but of all time; they would point also to the scope and quality of *As I Lay Dying, Light in August* and *Absalom, Absalom!* When one considers the good features of *Sartoris, Go Down Moses* and even the lurid *Sanctuary* it becomes apparent that Faulkner's claim to greatness is a substantial one. At the very least we must consider him as a writer of considerable talent, great originality and – though uneven – still significant achievements.

First among these is his strange and intense portrayal of the South:

> Then the honeysuckle got into it. As soon as I turned off the light and tried to go to sleep it would begin to come into the room in waves building and building up until I would have to get up and feel my way like when I was a little boy.

Even when Faulkner's characters try to escape, the atmosphere of the South is always with them, so much so that some critics have simply seen that it, rather than any person, is the chief character in his novels; and certainly Faulkner did become conscious late in his career that his novels could be read as one vast Southern chronicle – the story of Yoknapatawpha County, Northern Mississippi. We should not take the chronicle point too seriously

(Faulkner's authorial motives are too complex for that), but it is certainly true that he is the first writer of real literary stature since the Victorians to create and people a geographic world – a world which in this case is archetypally Southern. Michael Millgate writes:

> His deep identification with his own region is one of his greatest strengths, especially as it emerges in the marvellous sense of place, whether it be the heart of the wilderness or the interior of Miss Reba's brothel, and in the rich evocation of the world of Yoknapatawpha County; . . . certainly the intensity of his tragic power in novels such as *The Sound and the Fury*, *Light in August*, and *Absalom, Absalom!* derives both from this profoundly localised sense of social reality and from a poignant awareness of the proud and shameful history of the courageous, careless, gallant and oppressive South.

The South traditionally sees itself as being all the things Millgate describes – courageous, careless, gallant and repressive: it has not ducked facts that outsiders dislike, such as the treatment of Negroes; it admits, and takes a particular pride in admitting, what is for other people unpalatable. Faulkner's novels are themselves lists of admitted things, and the emotional conflict within them (a similarity to Updike) is how you learn to live with things you have admitted. In *Absalom, Absalom!*, for example, Quentin Compson at the end of the novel finds himself experiencing emotionally certain things which he has always intellectually admitted about the South. For Quentin, a whole series of contradictions demand resolution. His recounting of Thomas Sutpen's story to his Harvard room-mate Shreve is not exactly therapeutic (one senses little possibility of a cure) but it is diagnostic; Shreve does not know or understand the South, and he demands not merely that the amazing tale of Sutpen's rise and fall should be told but that it should be explained. In the explanation Quentin is forced to face the contradictions which he has accepted mentally but not emotionally; he has to accept his own confusion about the

South; above all he has to accept that 'the wistaria Mississippi summer, the cigar smell, the random blowing of the fireflies' also contains and perhaps needs the semi-savage force of a Thomas Sutpen. He must accept too that the incest and miscegenation which Sutpen trails after him are a part of Quentin's own heritage, a part that will not go away. At the end of the novel Shreve confronts Quentin with two deadly opinions about the South: first – a theme that occurs repeatedly in Faulkner – that it is a huge decaying anachronism; second, that Negroes and, therefore, miscegenation are here to stay, and that quite shortly the whole Western world will be pale coffee coloured. Shreve immediately follows this by asking Quentin why he hates the South, and gets a revealing reply:

> 'I don't hate it,' Quentin said, quickly, at once, immediately; 'I don't hate it,' he said. *I don't hate it*, he thought, panting in the cold air, the iron New England dark; *I don't. I don't! I don't hate it!* I don't hate it!

The speed of Quentin's reply shows that he *does*, that unconsciously he has been revealing all along to Shreve what previously he suppressed; at last he has to face up to the consequences of the South, to face what he feels about his own heritage; and the panic of the repeated 'don'ts' shows that he is now fully realising the presence of the terror. We know from *The Sound and the Fury* that Quentin is due to commit suicide, and at least part of the strain that causes it comes from his closeness to and dependence on the South clashing with his hatred for it. Thus, when we say that Faulkner's novels contain above all the South, we are not talking only of the vividness of his descriptions or of the typicality of his characters, we are talking about the creation of an atmosphere which is a psychological condition in itself.

This is not a feature that everyone likes. Faulkner's predecessor, the Virginian novelist Ellen Glasgow, suspected that his rendering of the South was souped up in order to correspond with the North's morbid and prurient curiosity, and is simply grotesque.

This criticism can be applied most validly to the depiction of the South in what is undoubtedly Faulkner's most lurid novel, *Sanctuary*. Here a young college lady, Temple Drake, mislaid by a drunken boyfriend, falls into the clutches of bootleggers and psychopaths. The prime psychopath, Popeye, is impotent and therefore resorts to deflowering Temple with a corn cob. He next transports her to an adjacent brothel and imports a stud to do what he, Popeye, cannot; whereupon the unfortunate Temple turns with improbable abruptness into a monster of slaveringly unfulfillable lust. Irrespective of any doubts we may have about the literal truth of such episodes (Leslie Fiedler comments that fortunately the book is not quite convincing enough to be bearable), there is still the direct connection drawn between this bizarre behaviour and the environment, as if in the South such horrors were par for the course.

If the novel was not deliberately sensational, written for the money, as Faulkner suggested – and it seems clear that it was not – is he revealing, however imperfectly, important truths about the South, or merely revelling self-indulgently in his own morbid fantasies? In his defence, we may point out that at least some of the sensational events which Faulkner describes in this and other novels actually happened. The horrible, almost ritual castration and murder of Joe Christmas in *Light in August* was probably based on the equally ghastly lynching of one Nelse Patten in 1908 in Oxford, Mississippi. Similarly the Temple Drake episode is supposedly based on a real story whose events were actually played down by Faulkner. I say 'supposedly' because I am unsure how far one can believe him; he certainly attempts to mislead over the revisions of *Sanctuary*, and despite the publication of a recent biography his character remains curiously opaque.

In Faulkner's defence, it must be noted how much his social description has in common with other Southern writers. Carson

McCullers, Flannery O'Connor, Eudora Welty, Katherine Anne Porter and Robert Penn Warren all portray a similar South full of violence, emotional inbreeding, claustrophobic attachment to the past, morbid sexuality and great geographic beauty.

Also we might point out that not only the South but the rest of America and, for that matter, the world have to live with acts of grotesque and terrible violence; it seems unfair to pick on Faulkner for portraying what is after all a local representation of an international phenomenon. Why, we might ask, is there so much critical attention given to the castration and death of Faulkner's Joe Christmas, and none whatsoever to the exactly similar death, in Dos Passos' *USA*, of Wesley Everett? The answer lies in the way the thing is done. In Dos Passos the event is presented barely – as if the facts were so terrible that to add anything more to them would be unbearable. In Faulkner the events are dwelt on by more than one character, and the telling takes page upon page.

But, in order to understand both Faulkner and his significance for the American novel, we need to take a closer look at two of what are recognised as his best works: *As I Lay Dying* and *The Sound and the Fury*.

As I Lay Dying is in many ways a masterpiece. As the novel opens, Addie Bundren, the mother of the family, is dying while the rest of the family prepare her coffin and get ready to take her body on the long journey to Jefferson to bury her 'among her own people'. The journey is fraught with problems: the river is too high – as is Addie Bundren's corpse; one of the sons turns into an incendiary; the daughter Dewey Dell is pregnant; her father Anse is determined to steal her savings (and abortion money) to buy himself a set of false teeth. Yet for all their oddity these characters are among the most successfully rounded that Faulkner ever created, largely due to the specific method of their presentation. The book is divided into a number of distinct sections, and framed entirely as interior monologue from each of the characters. The individuality, the intensely characteristic quality of each character's voice and thought patterns, represents an immense triumph for Faulkner, whose effort bears favourable comparison with Virginia Woolf's use of a similar technique in *The Waves*. There, although the differences between the characters are well established by the different things they say, there is a cloying similarity about the way in which they say them. Faulkner escapes this trap. Vardaman, the youngest son, is hypertonic and hysterical; starved of affection, and horrified at his mother's death, his speech has all the hysteria of the disturbed child who sees events and understands nothing about them except in so far as they hurt him. Thus, though he gets very upset when his mother's coffin is lost in the river ('. . . and Cash hollering to catch her and I hollering running and hollering . . .'), when Jewel's back is burned he reacts with wide-eyed non-comprehension:

> Jewel was lying on his face. His back was red. Dewey Dell put the medicine on it. The medicine was made out of butter and soot, to draw out the fire. Then his back was black. 'Does it hurt Jewel?' I said. 'Your back looks like a nigger's, Jewel.'

Vardaman's speech/thoughts are quite different from his brothers'. Darl is poetic and descriptive:

> Above the ceaseless surface they stand – trees, caves, vines – rootless, severed from the earth, spectral above a scene of immense yet circumscribed desolation filled with the voice of the waste and mournful water.

Jewel, who speaks only once, is full of furious intensity, while Cash speaks only about the practical, and in what he sees as the most practical way possible:

> 'I made it on the bevel.
> 1. There is more surface for the nails to grip.
> 2. There is twice the gripping surface to each seam.'

The point seems all the more impressive in view of the number of characters and voices in *As I Lay Dying* (many more than in *The*

Waves); and the vividness of the expression of so many of the characters who cross the Bundrens' path creates a whole series of – often comic – vignettes.

This interpenetration of character, atmosphere and narrative gives the book a distinctively intense flavour of its own. What Faulkner has achieved is some of the richly complex emotional reaction to events that is an integral part of life. The very end of the book is a splendid example of this. Anse appears with new teeth, followed by 'a kind of duck-shaped woman all dressed up' carrying a gramophone. Anse greets his family thus:

> 'It's Cash and Jewel and Vardaman and Dewy Dell' pa says, kind of hangdog and proud too, with his teeth and all, even if he wouldn't look at us. 'Meet Mrs Bundren,' he says.

The reader feels partly admiration – Anse has got his way as he always does; partly humour – Anse's preoccupation with teeth has recurred with quiet obsessiveness throughout the journey; partly frustration – that the purely selfish can always win because they care only for themselves; partly anger – he shouldn't get away with it; partly compassion – for the wrecked and exploited others who have done all the work, who have carried their mother's body all the way to see her replaced by a duck-shaped woman carrying a gramophone; and finally pity – not only for the mess that the Bundrens are in, with Dewey Dell still pregnant, Darl in an asylum, but because Anse's action shows that they are still trapped in the claustrophobic atmosphere of family feud and rural strife.

Yet, having praised *As I Lay Dying*, we should also recognise that it reveals some inconsistencies. For instance, although the characters, narrative and voice are good, there are moments of overwriting – as in Darl's description of Jewel on horseback:

> Then Jewel is enclosed by a glittering maze of hooves as by an illusion of wings; among them, beneath the upreared chest, he moves with the flashing limberness of a snake . . . Jewel with dry

heels, shutting off the horse's wind with one hand, with the other patting the horse's neck in short strokes and caressing, cursing the horse with obscene ferocity.

It is scarcely conceivable that a member of the Bundren family could think that. 'An illusion of wings'; 'short strokes myriad and caressing' – it is too literally hyperbolical. Nor is this problem restricted to Darl:

> 'It is dark. I can hear wood, silence: I know them. But not living sounds, not even him. It is as though the dark were resolving him out of his integrity, into an unrelated scattering of components – snuffings and stampings; smells of cooling flesh and ammoniac hair; an illusion of a co-ordinated whole of splotched hide and strong bones within which, detached and secret and familiar, an *is* different from my *is*.'

No amount of hypertension can account for Vardaman's gift of tongues. The very careful use of 'integrity' in its mathematical sense of 'whole', with the parallel use of 'resolving' in its original sense of re-forming, the immensely assured compression of thought in 'unrelated scattering of components', all show a degree of articulacy quite beyond Vardaman. Faulkner has taken over and, having done so, has been carried away with the sheer exultation of his own undoubted powers of description.

Disconcerting also is the chapter in which, *post mortem*, we are given a chunk of Addie's consciousness. The section is magnificently written. In seven pages Faulkner creates a devastatingly vivid picture of Addie's twisted and frustrated life; I do not think that, outside Dickens, there is any better rendering of that most terrible theme – cruelty to a child begetting twisted adult begetting more cruelty to more children. We understand and sympathise with Addie as we are repelled by her. Considered in isolation the section is a masterpiece, but considered in context it is very strange indeed. First, although Addie is dead, she is allowed to enter the book, speak and leave without any preamble or explanation. This is all the odder when we realise that Addie is in some senses the centre of the novel; she has held the family to-gether by main force and continues to do so until the very moment of her burial; and it is her personality, her character traits (more than Anse's) that are distributed among her children. If then this section of Addie's is intended to be thematically the centre of the novel, it is contextually speaking presented with inconsequent abruptness. Indeed the very absence of any atmospheric centring suggests that Faulkner may simply and arbitrarily have decided to give us another point of view.

But there is, I think, a more acceptable reason for the presenta-tion of this section – a reason which reflects interestingly on the whole nature of Faulkner's work. Addie's section is the most straightforward in the novel – not only does it spell out various details hinted at previously (for example, the guilty secret of Addie's lover and the fact of Jewel's illegitimacy) but it tells the story of Addie's life in a completely direct and sequential way; it also accompanies the narrative progression with a similarly clear, direct and sequential progression of motive. And, since this is so well done, one wonders why Faulkner did not do it more often; why are so many of the sections so elliptical, throwing out hints and suggestions, now approaching some events at a tangent only to withdraw at a tangent, now going over and over the same item of experience?

The answer is that Faulkner distrusts the straightforward be-cause it puts events and characters and the whole world in a context of order he does not want and does not believe in. Faulkner has an almost pathological distrust of structure. Con-sidered from this angle Addie's section ceases to be straight-forward and becomes merely another example of dissociation. The very complete and organised quality of the Addie section – abandoned as it is in the middle of the book – merely points up the futility of organising what is really disorganised, of explaining the inexplicable; given its surroundings, it too becomes dis-organised, inexplicable.

Often, too, the problem which confronts Faulkner's characters is not merely that of suffering from damaged or twisted emotions – though that happens in plenty – but that genuine or healthy emotions are denied their proper context, as if even the straightest plants must grow twisted in the Southern air. Thus, in *The Sound and the Fury*, we can trace the twisting of Caddie by her upbringing, and the failure of Dilsey's attempts to create a world of peace and order out of the collective psychotic impossibility that is the Compson family. Similarly, in *Light in August*, Byron Bunch's genuine desire to love and cherish fastens on the smugly self-absorbed figure of Lena Grove; while, in *As I Lay Dying*, the twisting process of Anse and Addie's marriage has resulted in varying degrees of emotional breakdown. Repeatedly the characters suffer not only from a crisis of identity – that is, not knowing who they are – but not knowing what they feel or, even more striking, what relationship there is between a given feeling and its object. Thus they pass through the book applying their dissociated emotions to inappropriate objects, attaching themselves to meaningless rituals – Jewel transfers his love to a horse, Vardaman to a fish. Darl says that the Bundrens' journey becomes a 'denial of the significance [it] should have affiirmed'. Yet that is bound to happen, the denial is there before they even start because none of them has any real relationship with Addie; the journey is thus not a symbol of respect or love but rather of attachment to a meaningless ritual.

In Faulkner's masterpiece, *The Sound and the Fury*, the dissociation becomes even more obvious; but before developing this point I will give a brief review of the book. There are four sections: the first is related by Benjy, the idiot; the second by the grossly disturbed Quentin; the third by the brutal and sadistic Jason; and the fourth – although it centres on the conduct of the Negro servant Dilsey and more or less presents events from her point of view – is narrated from the outside by the author. The sections are narrated at different times: while Quentin's is dated 2nd June

1910, Jason's, Benjy's and Dilsey's are dated respectively 6th, 7th and 8th April 1928, a chronology which, pointing as it does to Easter, has led critics into much discussion of Christian symbolism. It is typical of Faulkner that he should not present those three successive dates in successive chronological order – he wants, it would seem, no concessions to patterning or contextualising. It is also typical that his experiments with time do not stop there; in each of the sections the character ranges freely across time, imagining different events from different periods – a process which, in the Benjy and Quentin sections, results in an extraordinary temporal scrambling. Benjy the idiot has no sense of time; thus events from the past and the present are the same to him and come into his consciousness in no order but only as they are called forth by some form of association. So the calling out of 'Caddie' by a nearby golfer releases not only a flood-tide of feelings about his long-departed sister Caddie, but a flood as real and immediate as it was eighteen years before. Similarly Quentin, who is on the point of suicide and suffers from incest feelings for Caddie, is dementedly obsessed both with precise chronological time (his section is full of clocks and watches) and with the horror and meaninglessness of the world. So his mind runs events together, his emotions triggering off the memory of events irrespective of their place in a chronological time sequence.

The bare reporting of this technique cannot hope to reproduce the sheer density of the work as it confronts us. To put it simply, it is extremely difficult to find out what has happened or is happening, and it is only by carefully re-reading one's way backwards and forwards across the sections, and by comparing different references – often very glancing – to the same events, that the action emerges. We gradually put together the decline of the Compsons – the death of Mr Compson, the loss of Caddie's virginity, Quentin's suicide, the castration of Benjy and so on. However, admirers of *The Sound and the Fury* have always been quick to defend the novel against charges of obscurity, over-difficulty or over-experimentation. Its difficulty, they argue, is that of great art, and ultimately fully justified.

My own view is that, for all the novel's undoubted triumphs, there is a pull in it between the portrayal of experience and of the things experienced. Several of what are held to be the novel's themes: the lovelessness of the Compsons, the morality of the heart as against legalistic morality, man's capacity to endure, the need to abandon the past and live in the present – these are certainly to be found in the book. Yet I dispute that they have much to do with our experience as we read the book; what we *feel* is what it is like to be in whatever situation Faulkner is describing at that moment.

Speaking of Caddie, Faulkner said:

> . . . the girl was the only one that was brave enough to climb that tree to look in the forbidden window to see what was going on. And . . . it took the rest of the four hundred pages to explain why she was brave enough to climb the tree to look in the window. It was an image, a picture to me, a very moving one, which was symbolized by the muddy bottom of her drawers as her brothers looked up into the apple tree that she had climbed to look in the window. And the symbolism of the muddy bottom of the drawers became the lost Caddy . . .

Surely it does not take four hundred pages to explain why Caddie was brave enough; the firmness of her character, her presence as a strong whole living force is established early on, and continually reinforced by her treatment of Benjy. The explanation of Caddie's character is the least important thing in the book. What *is* important, however, is how the different characters – Quentin and Benjy particularly – feel about her, in turn taking the form of the images and pictures Faulkner speaks of. It is to these that he returns, it is for these that the themes exist – not the other way round.

When, for example, we finally come upon the explanation of an event which has previously puzzled us (the knowledge, for instance, that Benjy attempted to rape a young child and was castrated), our feeling is not one of intellectual pleasure at having discovered the truth, the point at last – as it often is in reading, say, Joyce – but an increased awareness of how Benjy felt at that time, in that situation.

Although explanation does often serve experience, there are occasions where it does not. While Faulkner is going over the same event from different viewpoints – *searching* (implicity or explicitly) for an understanding, an explanation of the event – he is convincing; but the closer he comes to that explanation the less convincing he is. He knows *how* people feel but not *why*, except on the most primitive of levels. We can accept, for example, that Quentin is as he is partly because of his father's weakness, coldness and misogyny. Yet, the more we hear (through Quentin) of the father's theories about life, explanations of Caddie's, Quentin's and human behaviour, the more the reader runs into danger of considering the idea on its own.

Paradoxically also, as long as an idea or an explanation can clearly be seen as unsatisfactory, then and only then can Faulkner make it convincing. This is illustrated by the last section of *The Sound and the Fury*, that which deals with Dilsey. Critics are often made very happy by the Dilsey section: it continues and increases the process of straightforward explanation begun by the preceding Jason section, thus confirming that the jigsaw pieces are in the right place; it introduces a note of normality; it says nice things about Negroes; and it allows one the apparent relief of plugging into comforting words like 'goodness' and 'endurance' – positive human values which have had a rough ride through the book so far, and in sadist Jason's section in particular. Yet, although Faulkner certainly intended Dilsey to be seen as a 'good human being [who] held the family together ... because it was the decent and proper thing to do ...', neither she nor her section provide any solution to or, for that matter, explanation of what has already happened. The male Quentin is dead, the brutal Jason is in charge and is torturing both Caddie and her daughter Quentin. Benjy, although cared for by Dilsey, still grieves intensely for Caddie and suffers at the hands of a succession of Negro 'minders'. The twisting of the female Quentin is only too likely to be transmitted to the next generation and, when Dilsey says of the Compsons, 'I've seed de first an de last', she is speaking no more than the truth. The ordered, structured world of Dilsey is not a solution to the chaotic worlds of the other Compsons, it is simply placed next to it.

Here it is well to notice something else which Faulkner wrote about the novel:

> . . . that's how the book grew. That is, I wrote that same story four times. None of them were right, but I had anguished so much that I could not throw any of it away and start over, so I printed it in the four sections. That was not a deliberate *tour de force* at all, the book just grew that way. That I was still trying to tell one story which moved me very much and each time I failed . . . And that's the reason I have the most tenderness for that book, because it failed four times.

Obviously the book can only be judged as a failure by the most exacting of standards, and Faulkner may well be speaking disingenuously when he puts the matter in those terms. However, I do think that his description of the work's genesis very much corresponds to the overall impression it makes. The four sections are good because they search and do not discover; they are good because the emotions churned over in them are suffered inexplicably, isolated, out of context; they are good because they reflect in their very texture Faulkner's honest incomprehension; and much of his art's success here comes from the portrayal of man desperately trying to find a context for the suffering he endures – and failing.

Yet what works in *The Sound and the Fury* does not always succeed so well elsewhere. It is fair to say that, from *The Unvanquished* onwards, the general view of Faulkner is of a writer who has passed his best and is creating work which is of interest but which possesses neither the force nor the originality of his greatest achievements. However, even in two of his more important novels, *Light in August* and *Absalom, Absalom!*, we can see some of the particular problems hinted at in *The Sound and the Fury*.

Both these books are genuinely extraordinary. The intensity they maintain, the sheer force that drives them on, is amazing. What they reflect also is the limited nature of the characters and feelings that Faulkner understands. In *Light in August*, for example, Joe Christmas thinks thus about his lover, the bizarrely perverted Joanna Burden:

> During the first phase it had been as though he were outside a house where snow was on the ground, trying to get into the house; during the second phase he was at the bottom of a pit in the hot wild darkness; now he was in the middle of a plain where there was no house, not even snow, not even wind.

What that expresses admirably is the nightmare state of being Joe Christmas – identifying with neither Negro nor white; the state of not even knowing whether one is Negro and/or white; the state of being a complete outcast, of being so warped in childhood that feeling itself becomes a threat; the state of utter desolation which, bordering on madness, leads Christmas to a psychopath's murder and a psychopath's death. This nightmare condition, this suffering on the limits of sanity, Faulkner understands well and conveys superbly; we also see it in so many of the novel's other characters, who are almost universally crazy.

Joe Christmas has already been described; to the litany of his individual horrors we might add the vicious rigours of his Calvinistic upbringing which help to produce the feeling that suffering is the only reality, so that he must kill in order to find it. But consider the other characters. Apart from the various disturbed people who brought Christmas up, we meet the Reverend Gail Hightower – he 'couldn't get religion and that galloping cavalry and his dead grandfather shot from the galloping horse unentangled from each other, even in the pulpit'; his entanglement with Southern ancestor worship drives him from the church and his wife to promiscuity and suicide. Consider Joanna Burden, who combines a fiercely menopausal passion for Negroes:

> Now and then she appointed trysts beneath certain shrubs about the grounds where he would find her naked, or with her clothing half torn to ribbons upon her, in the wild throes of nymphomania . . . with her wild hair each strand of which would seem to come alive like octopus tentacles, and her wild hands and her breathing: 'Negro! Negro! Negro!'

with a dignified interest in black charities. Consider the protofascist Percy Grimm who, steeped in his own mediocrity, can find power only in the megalomaniac pursuit, slaughter and dismemberment of Christmas. Consider even Byron Bunch, who appears so much more normal than the other characters, yet who is impotent, who can attach himself only to someone like Lena Grove with whom, pregnant by another – mad and repulsive – man, there can be no relationship. Our last view of Byron is of him dragging himself off across Alabama in the wake of the mindlessly fecund and archetypally selfish Lena Grove, smugly nursing the baby that 'had been eating breakfast now for about ten miles like one of these dining cars on the train'; the Lena who is 'just travelling' without giving a damn about Byron.

One could extend the list considerably, but at the least it introduces some doubts about the breadth of Faulkner's understanding of life and of people.

> The town looked upon them . . . as being a little touched – lonely, grey in colour, a little smaller than most other men or women, as if they belonged to a different race, species.

Even if Faulkner has as many technicolor characters as he has grey ones, many readers do feel that they (like Christmas' grandparents in that quotation) belong to a different species, that they are too Gothic to be convincing. Critics point out that, even when Faulkner attempts to show a 'normal' character, he never enters that character's consciousness as he does with his metaphorical Bedlam of madmen. Thus, in *The Sound and the Fury*, we see the positive qualities of Dilsey and Caddie only from the outside – either through authorial comment or the far from reliable perceptions of the other characters. In the majority of Faulkner's novels the nearest thing to normality we find is a character who still possesses some good instincts but is severely emotionally crippled or handicapped to the point of ineffectiveness by his surroundings.

Moreover, Faulkner's critics would argue, the 'disturbed' characters are not always presented fairly. The sympathy we feel for Christmas, or Hightower or Quentin Compson, is withheld unjustly from other characters. Jason Compson, for example, is a sadist, but he is so because of the deprivation of his background – exactly the same thing which has twisted Quentin. Yet Faulkner clearly feels for Quentin, while saying that Jason 'represented complete evil. He's the most vicious character in my opinion that I ever thought of . . .' It is a case of favouritism; Jason is undergoing moral taxation without spiritual representation.

So many of Faulkner's good qualities – his sense of comedy, his narrative gift, his powers of description, his knack with dialogue – either endure a segregated existence, living uneasily next to the obsessional areas that really concern him, or are distorted by them. What the reader must decide for himself is how far the novels transcend the sensations of the moment, and the limitations of the very narrow, twisted world they describe, and achieve validity as a common – and perhaps particularly modern example of – human experience.

JOHN UPDIKE

Updike is in wordly terms a successful writer. He has always taken pride in the professionalism of his work – at one point he said he would rather write the labels on sauce bottles than take another job. His novels have for the most part enjoyed a wide and varied readership, and as far as the general public goes his name is well known. However, neither intellectually nor academically is he as well thought of as he might be. Though he does not lack academic attention, all too often he is seen as slick, rhapsodic, glossy and middlebrow. While I think those criticisms are not entirely groundless, and am of the opinion that he has not come close to fulfilling his real promise, there is a great deal to be said for him as a writer of what is both good and representational in the modern American novel.

I shall look at Updike's richest books: *Rabbit Run, Couples* and *Rabbit Redux*. Readers should also take note of *The Poorhouse Fair, The Centaur* and *Bech: a Book* – each of them has its own good points; but this is hardly the case with the latest two, rather desperate novels (*A Month of Sundays* and *Marry Me*) which have most of his faults and few of his virtues.

Updike's works, like Faulkner's, reveal an increasing unease with structure, whether in form or content; in Updike's case this shows particularly in the concentration on perception as a last desperate remedy for the problem of meaninglessness. Again and again, like so many modern novelists, he returns to describe and evoke experience – no matter what that experience may be – for, in the face of increasing social and personal collapse, the feeling of the moment is the only positive reality man has. Of course, his novels contain other elements, but their real texture and force come from the linking of moments of intense experience – for again it is only in these moments that his characters know they are alive. In *Rabbit Run* the hero, stultified by his job demonstrating a foul kitchen implement called the MagiPeel Peeler, tries to recall the ecstasy of his experiences as a high-school basketball star having an affair with a prostitute, Ruth. At the end of the book – after a series of what are either misfortunes or blunders depending on the extent of your sympathy for Rabbit, after the death of his younger child, reunions and breakups with his wife, after his cruel rejection of Ruth (he makes her turn prostitute tricks on him, though she loves him and clearly hates the idea) – he returns to discover that she is pregnant. His reaction is interesting. He is horrified at the thought that she might have had an abortion and, despite the mess he is in, is delighted, ecstatically delighted, that she has not. Yet when Ruth puts a series of practical questions to him – will he divorce his wife, will he marry her, what will he do? – all Rabbit can say is, 'I don't know'. Afterwards, running away again, he thinks to himself:

> Funny, how what makes you move is so simple and the field you must move in so crowded. His legs take strength from the distinction, scissor along evenly. Goodness lies inside, there is nothing outside, those things he was trying to balance have no weight. He feels his inside as very real suddenly, a pure blank space in the middle of a dense net. *I don't know*, he kept telling Ruth; he doesn't know, what to do, where to go, what will happen, the thought that he doesn't know seems to make him infinitely small and impossible to capture.

The only thing Rabbit knows is how he feels; he does not understand external circumstances, the hard facts of his or Ruth's plight, the arguments about the rights and wrongs of the situation with the clergyman Eccles; the only right or good he can understand is the ecstasy of the moment. And it is interesting that in *Rabbit Run* we have the forerunner of something which comes to obsess Updike in *Couples* and *Rabbit Redux* – namely, the ecstasy to be got from inverting experience. Like some latter-day Huysmans, Rabbit deliberately desecrates his sacramental experience with Ruth. (I think this is a process still unresolved in Updike; as in Lawrence's *Lady Chatterley's Lover*, he manifests the contrary desires to shock the reader with the 'secret' knowledge of perversion and then to convince him that because it is knowledge it is not perverse.)

Updike's concern with the relationship between intense experience and morality receives a much more detailed treatment in *Couples*. The hero, Piet Hanema, lives in an affluent and outflung New England community neatly called Tarbox (Updike is very good at names – a good gauge of an author's talent). Tarbox is not a suburb, but it is becoming one, a process which Piet, partner in the building firm of Gallagher and Hanema, is steadily accelerating by erecting uninteresting, profitable, jerry-built houses – very different from those period dwellings where Piet and his neighbours live:

> He had grown to love this house, its rectangular low rooms, its baseboards and chair rails molded and beaded by hand, the slender mullions of the windows whose older panes were flecked with oblong bubbles and tinged with lavender . . .

It would not be wholly distorting to say that everyone in Tarbox is having an affair with everybody else and, although Piet is undoubtedly the central character and his the central affairs, one of the novel's practical problems is the meandering excursions Updike takes into the other characters' sexual diversions. Updike's treatment of sex in this novel has led him to be accused of pornography – there is so much sex and it is described in such, almost gloating, detail. Yet his intention is not pornographic. He goes over different sex between different people to discover what sex is. What is it this experience that is so important; why do we do it; why do we want to do it; *do* we want to do it? One is reminded of Faulkner's hypnotic waltzing round and round the subject, stressing by each return to it the importance of the same questions. Again like Faulkner, Updike is concerned with what the experience of sex means in relation to other experiences, and the various meanings we put upon them.

In Updike this concern is superficially more straightforward. His characters say out loud what Faulkner's never could; yet, as *Couples* goes on, we realise that things are not as simple as they seem. Even if Updike does not treat with incest and sexually intense violence, sex in *Couples* becomes more and more twisted; and the unsatisfactory nature of sex as a substitute for all that is wrong in life – and especially in American society – becomes evident. Piet, whose first affair with Georgene originally possessed a joyful, even an innocent quality, finds not even that the whole thing has gone sour on him but merely that he has lost interest. Exactly the same process – although to a much more serious degree – takes place in his affair with Foxy which begins as strangely tender and ends as strangely nasty. The key fact here is that, before the affair starts, Foxy is pregnant by her husband, the cold, distant and narcissistic Ken – whose only relationship is with his scientific research. Updike thus becomes one of the few writers to describe a not uncommon phenomenon – which many writers squeamishly shun – a sexual relationship with a pregnant woman. The fact that she is pregnant upsets the other couples in the book, much as it probably upsets squeamish writers, but Updike must be given great credit for the tenderness and affection which his portrayal of their love-making evokes. But, once Foxy has given birth, Piet does not really want her: '. . . in giving birth without notifying him, she had been guilty of an affront and in that guilt promised him freedom'. Setting aside for the moment how we should read certain scenes at the end of the novel, Piet subsequently shows real interest in Foxy only on one extra-ordinary occasion when he catches her in the bathroom at a party and gets her to let him suck her breasts.

> 'Nurse me.'
> 'Oh darling. No.'
> 'Nurse me.'
> She covered one breast, alarmed, but he had knelt, and his broad mouth fastened on the other. The thick slow flow was at first suck sickeningly sweet.

There is something unbalanced about Piet's sexual obsession with pregnancy, and we can also see that his sexual experiences are be-coming increasingly isolated and selfish. Indeed, if the affection and joy which Piet has given Foxy has turned into this, we see that his is really a barbaric exploiting tenderness of the sort Lawrence was always quick to portray in the characters he disliked. Thus the healing restorative quality which Updike's characters seek in the sexual experience seems to be not only transitory but in the end destructive, itself reasserting the very confusion and unhappiness it sought to solve. Sex, which was 'good' to Piet, becomes in the end for him what it is to the other couples – something to pass the time, to ward off boredom, to occupy the blank meaningless space between adolescence and senility in a blank meaningless universe.

This blankness and meaninglessness is illustrated by the other alternatives to sex that Updike offers. Among these, religion and politics are paramount. Like Faulkner, Updike is obsessed with religion, or rather with religions. He himself said that the question his novels are posing is 'after Christianity what?', and he always introduces religion early on. In *Rabbit Run*, for example, we are told in the first few chapters that Rabbit and his wife Janice are Christians, and the interest in and influence on their problems which the clergyman Eccles is allowed to take illustrates a particularly American phenomenon – the continuing conventional importance of religion in American life. Americans are after all a church-going people; an American Sunday morning is active with people going to church, in a way that is still observable in Europe only in the more militantly Catholic countries. This is partly an historical phenomenon; America's foundations are built on the search for freedom of worship, and the importance of a church as a social centre to a frontier society is obvious. Something of this importance persists to the present day; when an American television announcer late on Saturday evening says, 'See you in church tomorrow', he is expressing a whole series of social feelings: pride in the fact of religious toleration (in America you can worship where you want); an acknowledgement of the extent to which his listeners are inhabitants of God's own country; but, above all, a sense of historical community, the exhortation to meet and celebrate the traditional straightforward mystery of being an American. Although the twentieth-century novel is always concerned with religion (one only has to think of Waugh, Greene and Forster in England, Gide and Mauriac in France), it is manifested in a particularly straightforward – some would say primitive – form in the American novel of the period. To appreciate the spiritual dilemmas of Greene's or Gide's characters, we need at least a fair understanding of theology; to understand, say, Faulkner's, we need only relate to the most evident human flaw. For example, the Reverend Gail Hightower shares with Greene's Scobie (in *The Heart of the Matter*) a split between his human desires and his religious training. Yet, because Hightower's problem is presented as quintessentially a Southern social one, we need very little understanding of his actual religious beliefs; his problem is, indeed, more human than it is religious, and our reaction to the loss of his church at the hands of his morally censorious congregation is a reaction to a personal and social problem rather than a wide-rangingly theological or cosmically spiritual one. Yet even intelligent students reading Greene cannot appreciate Scobie's dilemma – indeed, cannot see that there is a dilemma – unless they know something of Catholic theology concerning the Eucharist.

Thus, when Updike introduces the Church into his novels, he is dealing with a local historico/social as well as a universal religious phenomenon. (The Congregational church in Tarbox, which Piet watches burn down, is deliberately described as a masterpiece of eighteenth-century craftsmanship, all that Tarbox itself originally represented.)

Thus also the loss of religious meaning is seen as the loss of traditional American social meaning. This is apparent early on in *Couples* when we learn (via Freddy Thorne, the demon dentist – one of Updike's best and saddest characters) that the couples have made themselves into a church. And this theme is re-emphasised

96

by the fact that Piet and Foxy, two of the characters who take religion and church attendance at all seriously, are the two who, by their affair, break the 'rules'; for Foxy's abortion (of Piet's child) and her divorce upset the equilibrium of adultery-within-marriage on which the rules of the couples' games depend.

But religion does not provide meaning any more than sex does. For one thing, it does not greatly affect the characters' lives; it does not seem to Piet and Foxy to have anything directly to do with their affair, and Matt Gallagher (Piet's business partner) 'secured his wife and only child behind a wall of Catholicism', a process that entails moral double-think. In business, 'He dreamed of corrupting whole hillsides, yet wished to keep himself immaculate', and while smugly lecturing Piet on morality he turns a very blind eye to his wife's affair. The other Catholic couple, the Ongs, though less unpleasant, are not much of an advertisement for the significance of religion. John Ong, dying of cancer, loses his faith; and at a party his wife, Bernadette, makes what passes for a pass at Piet.

> Bernadette, her body wrapped in silk, a toy gold cross pasted between her breasts, heard a frug record put on the phonograph and held wide her arms; Piet saw her dying husband in her like a larva in a cocoon.

Readers will not fail to notice that the cross is 'toy'.

Politics is equally ineffective as an alternative. It, like the question of religion or the fear of death, haunts and punctuates the characters and their actions. Two obvious examples are the Cuban missile crisis and the assassination of John Kennedy. In the former case, Piet goes to play golf with a friend.

> They teed off into an utterly clear afternoon and between shots glanced at the sky for the Russian bombers. Chicago and Detroit would go first and probably there would be shouts from the clubhouse when the bulletins began coming in . . . As Americans they had enjoyed their nation's luxurious ride and now they shared the

privilege of going down with her . . . Driving home he heard on
the car radio that the Russians had submitted to inspection and
been allowed to pass. He had felt dismay that they must go on, all
of them, towards an untangling less involuntary and fateful.

On the night of Kennedy's death, the Thornes hold the party they
had already planned and the couples stand about being awkwardly
clever, unable to ignore or to mourn, wondering embarrassedly
what it has to do with them. In the earlier case, it is an extremely
strong guilt which requires a world holocaust for its expiation;
in the latter, the couples feel the weight of a public yet personal
guilt which they can neither shrug off nor accept.

Throughout *Couples* we hear of the growing American involve-
ment in Vietnam; in *Rabbit Redux* the theme continues (one of the
achievements of Updike's writing is that he can make Harry into
a 'hawk' on Vietnam *because* of his sensitivity – and make us
believe it). In both books, politics intersect with the characters'
lives only to make them appear more terrifyingly inexplicable.
The death of Jackie Kennedy's infant son increases the death
trauma of Piet's disturbed younger daughter. In *Rabbit Redux*,
while most of the characters stare uncomprehendingly at the news
of the day ('Springer is shaking his head over the York riots.
"Sniper fire four nights in a row, Harry. What is the world
coming to?" ') the Negro, Skeeter, speaks longingly of the war he
fought in Vietnam because it is the perfect anarchic and meaningless experience for which America is headed. What we are finding
here is in each case the inversion of essential Americanism; the
country in which the individual in society had his great chance –
and therefore in which society had its great chance – seems to have
lapsed into muddle. At the Tarbox Town Meeting (an historically
honourable American institution in which individual and society
traditionally adjust to each other's needs) Piet thinks as follows:

> Politics bored Piet. The Dutch in his home region had been ex-
> cluded from, and had disdained, local power. His family had been
> Republican under the impression that it was the party of anarchy;

they had felt government to be an illusion the governed should not encourage.

Very significant; the looseness of American socio-political life, the freedom which one could ignore and treat ironically as 'anarchy', has turned on a national scale into something approaching just that. Thus the town meeting – itself a symbol of America's thrusting purposeful meaningful approach to life – has been turned into a pointless exercise of 'self-righteous efficiency . . . hazed by booze'.

After considering at such length meaninglessness and its relation to experience, one should notice Updike's own tendency to opt out of any final, definite impression left by his books. He likes to see his novels as open-ended, a fact that sometimes bothers his critics. He has made it plain that the end of *Couples* is ambiguous:

> Now, though it has not been many years, the town scarcely remembers Piet, with his rattly pick-up truck full of odd lumber, with his red hair and corduroy hat and eye-catching apricot windbreaker . . . Angela . . . is still seen around, talking with Freddy Thorne on the street corner, or walking on the beach with a well-tailored wise-smiling small man, her father. She flew to Juarez in July and was divorced in a day. Piet and Foxy were married in September. Her father, pulling strings . . . found a government job for his new son-in-law, as a construction inspector for federal jobs, mostly military barracks in the Boston-Worcester area. Piet likes the official order and the regular hours. The Hanemas live in Lexington, where, gradually, among people like themselves, they have been accepted, as another couple.

On the one hand, the effect is sadly elegiac; on the other, Piet and Foxy have become another couple, with – Updike implies – the possibility of growth as well as decay. This possibility is seen also in the treatment of science in the novel. Although several of the male characters are to varying extents concerned with science, it is in the character of Ken Whitman, Foxy's husband, that it receives its most thorough treatment. His marriage to his work clearly makes him inadequate in human terms – 'He has never,' says Foxy 'been very curious about life, above the molecular level' – but she is not right in saying that his career is 'to demonstrate how mechanical life is'. It would be pointless here to go into detail about his work (that Updike does so is another sign of his amazing specificity, his far-ranging liveliness), except to say that Ken has the true scholar's passionate concern with life at the elemental level, and early in the book:

> ... longed to approach the mysterious heart of CO_2 fixation – chlorophyll's transformation of visible light into chemical energy. But here at life's ultimate chamber, the lone reaction that reverses decomposition and death, Ken felt himself barred.

There is too much specialised knowledge in the way. Yet at the end of the novel we learn that 'he thinks he's on to something significant. He's back on starfish', and that Foxy may well be right when she says to Piet, 'Compared to Ken you are primitive. The future belongs to him or to chaos.' In other words, Ken is the only one likely to uncover the meaning of or a meaning in life. He may possess the answer which Piet, with his simple terrified faith in the experience of the individual, cannot provide.

The fact of Ken's work therefore introduces the possibility of life as meaningful at the end of the novel; the optimistic reader may find in Piet's marriage to Foxy, and in the rebuilding of the church, the hopefulness inherent in life's capacity to absorb, change, mutate and continue. The church fits in neatly with this, for while 'the rumor in town is that the new building will not be a restoration but a modern edifice, a parabolic poured-concrete tent-shape peaked like a breaking wave', the builders *have* rescued the rooster/weathercock that surmounted the original building.

A similar open-endness can be found in *Rabbit Run* and *Rabbit Redux*. The passage previously quoted from the end of *Rabbit Run* makes the point, for one can debate how much Rabbit 'not knowing' constitutes a criticism. And at the very end:

He wants to travel to the next patch of snow. Although this block of brick three-storeys is just like the one he left, something in it makes him happy; the steps and window-sills seem to twitch and shift in the corner of his eye, alive. The illusion trips him. His hands lift of their own and he feels the wind on his ears even before, his heels hitting heavily on the pavement at first but with an effortless gathering out of a kind of sweet panic growing lighter and quieter, he runs. Ah: runs. Runs.

Clearly the lyrical use of 'runs' is attempting to capture the complexity of our feelings about Rabbit, and – as I have suggested earlier – the ratio of sympathy to impatience will depend on our own individual reactions to the character. More difficult to decide is whether we see his running as a sign of the essential meaninglessness of his existence or as a celebration, in the midst of chaos, of his sense of life.

Much the same question arises in *Rabbit Redux*, the novel in which Updike describes Rabbit's life ten years after the end of *Rabbit Run*. In the course of this, Janice leaves Harry (he is rarely called 'Rabbit' here – a sign of the increasing distance from his basketball days) and goes to live with a car salesman, Stavros. Harry picks up Jill, an adolescent upper-class runaway, who brings along with her a somewhat professionally demented Negro, Skeeter, recently returned from Vietnam and wanted by the police. They move in with Harry and his thirteen-year-old son, Nelson. From this point on, Updike's writing reaches and stays on a plane of orgasmic intensity, as the characters lock themselves into a white-hot debate about American society, and the demonic Skeeter preaches his gospel of destruction, starting with Jill to whom he gives drugs. Harry's neighbours, objecting to this irregular menage, burn the house with the drugged Jill inside. After this – towards the end of the novel – Mim, Rabbit's brash and tarty sister, arrives; and, in briefly pinching Stavros from Janice, provides the catalyst for Janice's reunion with Harry. Mim also says something significant to Harry when he speaks of his letting Jill die. (Throughout the novel Jill asks for Harry's help, asks him to get Skeeter thrown out of the house and to stop him giving her drugs; he always evades this, saying that she likes what is done to her, and on the night of the fire he behaves in a fatuously hesitant way, wanting to be told that she *must* have escaped rather than making the firemen get on with the job of rescuing her.) Mim says:

> 'She let herself die. Speaking of that, that's what I do like about these kids: they're trying to kill it. Even if they kill themselves in the process . . . The softness. Sex, love; me, mine. They're doing it in . . . They're burning it out with dope. They're going to make themselves hard clean through. Like, oh, cockroaches. That's the way to live in the desert. Be a cockroach. It's too late for you, and a little late for me, but once these kids get it together there'll be no killing them. They'll live on poison.'

At first sight that looks like a prophecy of nastiness and despair – self-destructiveness, living only at the expense of the death of the emotions in a world that is anyway a desert. Yet perhaps that death is necessary, perhaps it contains the seeds of another sort of life. After all, Harry has always been too weak and sentimental about emotions, and his weakness, like all weaknesses, is selectively cruel in its indulgence. In *Rabbit Run* everyone suffers because he wavers about in the face of different emotional appeals. In *Rabbit Redux* he will not throw Skeeter out because the police will get him, with the result that Jill suffers. At the same time though, Harry is always quick to engage in a different form of emotional softness, taking responsibility for everything, so that in the warm blanket of collective guilt he need never take action on individual issues. Thus, for Mim to say that Jill killed herself is another form of salutary burning, the forcing of Harry to admit that people can take responsibility. And, if Harry can absorb this in terms of his own character, perhaps there is some hope for him and Janice.

But, although there is more than one way to read the end, and therefore to interpret the whole of an Updike novel, I am not finally convinced. As with Faulkner, the coherent interpretations which may be placed upon the book do not adequately express the impression that the work itself makes. As with Faulkner, there is a strange dissonance between what the book talks about (its ideas and issues and themes) and what it *is* about (the feelings it engenders and obsessively returns to).

Here the question of guilt arises. We have already seen Piet's guilt that needs a world war to be exorcised and we have seen how Mim's advice to Harry involves advice about avoiding the sentimental indulgence of guilt. But even these examples do not convey the very wide-ranging presence of the emotion in all three of the novels under discussion, nor the twisted way in which it continually emerges. For Updike's central characters are both in pursuit of and in flight from guilt, a process which involves a distortion of experience – particularly sexual and religious experience – and of whatever meaning they are seeking. Thus, Rabbit both wishes to take on himself guilt for what is wrong with everything and everybody, and, having taken on the responsibility, wants – as we have seen in his treatment of Ruth – to escape from it. One questions (as in the case of Faulkner's characters) how representative the feelings of a character so obsessed can really be, and indeed how far the author understands or can cope with an emotion in which he himself appears to be deeply involved.

Piet provides a good example of this. All his feelings float up from a sea-bed of guilt, and this colours and distorts his attitude to religion and to sex. In church, 'Piet wondered what barred him from the ranks of those many who believed nothing. Courage, he supposed. His nerve had cracked when his parents died.' Piet's belief is mixed up with the fear of death, and guilt about the death of his parents in particular. The circumstances of this guilt are interesting, for what Piet actually worries about is that he was enjoying sex while they died in a car crash. Clearly a guilt of this strength involving sex with death starts much earlier than young manhood. This is consonant with the infantility of Piet's sexuality, as evidenced by his sucking child-like at Foxy's breast. And Piet and Foxy being married at the end is not going to change his guilt or his disturbance; it does not answer any of the real emotional problems that are raised. Updike himself is half-conscious of this, as shown by the strange presence of psycho-analysis in *Couples*. Despite Piet's rather heartless opposition, his wife Angela goes to an analyst and uncovers a certain number of things about the relationship between her childhood and her sex life. Several of the other characters experiment with psycho-analysis and, like all good educated middle-class Americans, they use – often half in jest – Freudian terms. Updike's attitude to this is not clear; one does not know whether he thinks there is anything in it or not. This confusion is especially significant, of course, in a novel in which the characters suffer from a wide variety of intense Freudian guilts.

How do these points affect the overall impression of the novels? This remains an atmosphere of frenzied and increasingly guilty intensity about life in general and sex in particular, with a gap developing between the ideas or issues, which concern the characters, and their emotions. In *Rabbit Redux*, for example, the reader increasingly loses his grip on the ideological debate between Harry, Skeeter and Jill, which supposedly forms the centre of the book, and increasingly finds that the moral issues being raised are not really what matter – what does grip the reader is the almost mad obsessiveness of the description.

The discrepancy between authorial intention and execution is also seen in Updike's use of symbol. Richard Poirier, in his interesting study of earlier American literature, *A World Elsewhere*, speaks of characteristic American writing which 'exists not to be clarified but as a kind of drama of the search for clarity, that symbols, myths and summaries are themselves only stabs in the dark'. A stab in the dark is exactly what a symbol is, but a stab which penetrates, which makes us albeit partially and sometimes minimally aware of the existence of profound forces beneath our actions and our apprehensions. Now, when the nineteenth-century American novel succeeds in using symbols, it is because that use (as in Melville) makes us aware of our own unawareness, brings into our consciousness terrors and joys buried in our unconscious. And the successful nineteenth-century novel, such as Twain's *Huckleberry Finn*, is one in which the narrative can convincingly and unforcedly permit the symbols to recur and live.

However, as time passes, the relationship between narrative and symbol becomes less easy. Again the reasons are lengthily complex, but one which can be quickly identified is a growth in self-consciousness. The writer who is conscious that he is using a symbol, or alternatively of what it is his symbols stand for, is in danger of losing some of his spontaneous force; his symbols become ideas, and his narrative either splits away from them or has to be mechanically twisted to accommodate them. Both of these particularly twentieth-century problems apply to Updike, and to a lesser extent to Faulkner. When the church burns down in *Couples*, many readers object not because it is a symbol but because Piet is too conscious of it as such. Watching it burn is not traumatic; it is simply watching an idea burn. Similarly, Updike's really spectacular skill as a narrator, his capacity to grip us by the sequence of events, becomes twisted by the need for the events to *mean* things; a symbolic significance which can only be found, never (except in an entirely stylised work) placed.

What interests me here with regard to the twentieth-century American novel in general and Updike in particular is the consequences to narrative. Updike is, like Fitzgerald, a novelist of traditional talents, and several recent critics have pointed this out. Charles Samuels, for example, in his brief study speaks of ours as a literary period of apocalyptists who destroy 'fabricated worlds' and 'symbolists taking off for nowhere from nothing', but says that Updike offers the novel's 'traditional pleasures', bringing freshness to the familiar while through concreteness making familiar the previously unknown. And Updike's means are traditional: the creation of character, the use of narrative – areas in which he achieves considerable success. While we may find limitations to his creation of character – sometimes he invents too many, sometimes he tries to take them deeper than he understands – he undoubtedly has an immensely sure grasp of the most traditional aspects of character.

In narrative, too, Updike shows great power and skill. We are driven forward at a cracking pace, sometimes even against our will. Even in the pretentious *The Centaur*, which suffers from a severe prolapse of the poetic faculty, we still want to know what is going to happen next. Yet, as with Faulkner, there is something strange about the relationship between narrative and the novel as a whole. We can see how, for example, in *Light in August*, Faulkner tells a whole series of stories – begins with the story of one character, tells it at great length and with great skill, then abandons it to begin another and pick up the first much later. This relates, of course, to my point about Faulkner and his dislike of an ordered context. This applies also to Updike; in *Couples* or *Rabbit Redux* we have the stories of several characters and, at the same time, a pull between the story of the character and the meaning which the author wishes to convey in it.

Here we find one of the great problems of the twentieth-century novel in general and the American form in particular – namely, that the traditional tools of the novelist, character and narrative, which were in the nineteenth century naturally allied to meaning, now have to be forced either because they no longer have a meaning to convey or because they are no longer an adequate medium of communication. So we find the traditional artistic impulse to communicate, coupled with the fear that communication is either meaningless or impossible.

This has far-reaching consequences; it may account for the crisis of confidence often found in modern novels, and especially for the abrupt abandonment or unconvincing completion of books that are promisingly begun. It may also account for the way in which the twentieth-century American novel has for many writers become a search, as if in the use of traditional skills a new tradition may emerge, as if through the very process of writing about life, life may reveal the secret of why we write about it – the secret of its lost meaning.

CHAPTER 3

Fantasy

In any century, fantasy involves a pronounced movement away from what the writer feels to be the general notion of reality; it allows the imagination to move towards a counter-world, whether it be inside or outside man. Many of the writers of the nineteenth century were unashamedly fantastic. We need only think of Poe, or of Melville's *Moby-Dick*, which bears the same relation to a normal whaling expedition as does Coleridge's 'Ancient Mariner' to a fjord cruise off Norway.

In my earlier discussion of the American dream, I described the peculiarly American association between the practical and the magical, suggesting that, on the one hand, America offers what were (and on an international level still are) magical possibilities; on the other hand, these are supposedly obtainable by practical means – hard work, self-help, strive-and-succeed. Yet, since this cannot possibly work for everyone, the practical is always on the look-out for magical aid. Hence the extraordinary liturgy of American advertising which continually offers some new form of transubstantiation – seven-stone weakling into President of the United States. The traditionally aspiring young American, with both practical and fantastic thoroughness, turns over every frog in case it metamorphoses into a princess. As Hollywood shows, for America no flight of fancy need be excessive, for there is always a touch of fantasy in the way it sees itself. (An interesting corollary of this can be found in J. D. Salinger's amusing but superficial *Catcher in the Rye* where the real problem of the adolescent hero, Holdon Caulfield, is that there is no fantasy world enduring enough to afford him the excitement that his imagination craves.)

For the sake of argument I have grouped the authors discussed in this chapter into three loose but informative categories: the mystical, the literary, and the social. My mystical writers – Henry Miller, William Burroughs, Jack Kerouac – share an almost Coleridgean belief in the value of heightened perceptions; a belief which carries with it a quasi-Messianic concern with the outermost limits of man's controllable experience: sex, drugs, drink; a belief which each uses to revive and localise a traditional American myth – that of the mystic traveller, the Whitmanesque drifter.

HENRY MILLER

Enter Henry Miller, and what an entry. It is no surprise that Miller is beloved of French intellectuals – his literary career beginning with the abandonment of his job as employment manager for Western Union at the age of forty and going on to be middle-agedly down and artistically out in Paris – has more than a touch of Gauguin or the Douanier Rousseau. It is, however, typical of Miller's inherent Americanism that so much of his work deals with the reasons for his decision – the details of his life in America as they are unveiled in *Black Spring* and in his trilogy *Sexus*, *Plexus* and *Nexus*. While it is currently fashionable to concentrate on these, rather than on the more outrageous *Tropic of Cancer* (or its follow-up *Tropic of Capricorn*), it is in *Tropic of Cancer* that the quintessential Miller is to be found; it is in this novel that his mystical side is most neatly encapsulated and exercises its greatest influence.

> Wherever there are walls there are posters with bright venomous crabs heralding the approach of cancer. No matter where you go,

no matter what you touch, there is cancer and syphilis. It is written in the sky; it flames and dances, like an evil portent. It has eaten into our souls and we are nothing but a dead thing like the moon.

That is the message of this extraordinarily forceful, sometimes very funny and sometimes naïvely childish book, which consists entirely of vignettes from Miller's Paris experiences. First, Miller sees walls everywhere; second, he sees the fact of the world's horror as an apocalyptic and therefore mystical revelation; third, his vision is one of death. As so many libidinous schoolboys know, Miller is a 'dirty' writer – not to grant him this would be to deny his very real force. He wants to horrify and shock just as much as he can; his favourite medium is the human body, in particular its sexual functions: 'When I look down,' he says, 'into this fucked-out cunt of a whore I feel the whole world beneath me, a world tottering and crumbling, a world used up and polished like a leper's skull.'

Well, many would argue that a whore's cunt is not the most reliable of perspectives; and, looked at through it, how does one expect the world to appear? Miller does not care; his concern is not to argue or to justify but to compel one to share his monomaniac and mystic vision, through which he wishes to attack convenient notions of optimism – to him all notions of optimism are convenient. But the thing Miller hates most about bourgeois reality is the absence of the ecstatic, the mystical experience.

In the four hundred years since the last devouring soul appeared, the last man to know the meaning of ecstasy, there has been a constant and steady decline of man in art, in thought, in action. The world is pooped out: there isn't a dry fart left. Who that has a desperate, hungry eye can have the slightest regard for these existing governments, laws, codes, principles, ideals, ideas, totems and taboos? If anyone knew what it meant to read the riddle of that thing which today is called a 'crack' or a 'hole', if anyone had the least feeling of mystery about the phenomena which are labeled 'obscene', this world would crack asunder.

No quotation could better represent Miller's philosophy. The world is finished because it has lost track of ecstasy; the sexual experience is seen as obscene while it is the world itself that is so; man should abandon himself to mystery instead of – by implication – living a repressively structured existence; man's sexual failure is bound up with the failure of his world as a whole; in so totteringly rotten a structure, the best thing that can be provided is a hard shove, the most constructive action is to be destructive.

Although Miller's mode of expression may be outlandishly brisk – particularly when we remember that *Tropic of Cancer* was published as long ago as 1934 – the message is, almost to the last detail, familiar. In Lawrence's *Women in Love*, Birkin made the same points in a similarly frenetic tone of voice. Nor do the parallels stop there. Both attack conventional education, and above all its idea – consciousness; both are fascinated and repelled by the mechanical forces of the world; both are terrified at the prospect that the mushiness and feebleness of humanity must lead to man's developing a self-protective inhumanity; both occasionally imagine a world in which man has vanished absolutely (Miller envisages a peopleless world of streets, Lawrence one inhabited only by rabbits!). Such a comparison flatters Miller, but it does point up the universality of the issues involved. And, certainly in the relationship between sex and society, Lawrence establishes his credentials far more successfully. Lawrence's sense of dread is always seen in a context, the surrounding world does not always feel what he feels; his horror and negativism is a part, not the whole of the world. Perhaps most striking of all, Miller replaces the obscenity of the 'real world' with another and personal obscenity; while Lawrence's characters, even at their most disgusted, recognise and are wracked by their own desire for dissent. They fight fire with fire, but not mud with mud.

The difference in Miller's reaction is a measure of his particularly American naïveté. His whole Paris trip is based on the knowledge that America is there in the background – a comfortably secure backdrop to react against. This manifests itself in a variety of ways. First, he is in Paris to write 'The Last Book', a work with a title which one might think self-explanatory until we learn that it will exhaust the age 'for a generation, at least'. Brief apocalypse! Elsewhere he rants that 'Men fall back on ideas, *comme d'habitude*. Nothing is proposed that can last more than twenty-four hours', not realising that the proposition that things last only twenty-four hours is itself an idea, and in fact that *his* whole book is idea-ridden. When he says that he loves 'everything that flows' and that everything turns out to be 'the urine that pours out scalding and the clap that runs endlessly', he is pushing across an idea as hard as any old-time American evangelist. Indeed, his idea about having no ideas has an especially cheerful American flavour. Being a tidy frontiersman he expresses very tidily the idea that there should be no frontiers. At times, too, he reveals a sudden and simple-mindedly nationalistic hero-worship, as in his abruptly introduced eulogy on Walt Whitman:

> ... Whitman, that one lone figure which America has produced in the course of her brief life ... Whatever there is of value in America Whitman has expressed, and there is nothing more to be said. The future belongs to the machine, to the robots. He was the Poet of the Body and the Soul ... What Europe has never had is a free, healthy spirit, what you might call a MAN. Goethe was the nearest approach ... [but] Goethe is an end of something, Whitman is a beginning.

Of course, there is much more to be said than that what Whitman expresses equals all American value – this is the vanity of the man who thinks he has come upon something startlingly clever. More interesting however, is his belief that, whatever else may be wrong with America, there is *an* American truth which Europe lacks, a truth to be found in one of her simplest and rawest writers, and a truth which is on-going. So Miller the prophet of doom is also Miller the prophet of possibility and freedom – concepts as American as Coca-Cola. It is not surprising,

therefore, that *Tropic of Cancer* ends with Miller considering returning to America, because spiritually he had never left it. Like
Christopher Isherwood in a more recent book, Miller is 'down
there on a visit' – 'there' is really 'down' but a tourist is still a
tourist and Miller's cancer can always get radio-therapy in a
Californian hospital.

The drift of that argument may be a little unfair; after all *Tropic
of Cancer* contains some magnificent comic vignettes. The Russian
princess who 'permitted' her lover to rape her is only one example
in a long line of excellently portrayed crooks and rogues. But
these cameos, together with the great forceful clarity of his prose
(has ever an unreadable book been more readable?), induce only a
feeling of regret – regret that we do not have something more
artistically complete than Miller's mauve memories, regret in a
sense that the true momentum of the book, its desire for ecstatic
revelation, does not have a broader or more concrete base.

WILLIAM BURROUGHS

A similar point applies to William Burroughs, in whose bizarre
and often boring books there are evidences of a powerful stylistic
gift – glimpses of something beautiful as it vanishes down an
elaborately decorated but still slimy drain. Burroughs is not – or
so it seems from experience with students – a writer to read as
much as one to rummage in. I am reminded of Wayne Booth who,
in discussing Joyce, said he did not want to give the impression
that he had read *Finnegan's Wake*, only that he had read *in* it. If,
however, this process engenders a sense of respectful wonder at
Joyce, it produces something less with Burroughs.

His popularity is understandable, certainly in an historical context. First, he writes about drugs, a specifically modern and
specifically modern American problem. Second, he writes about
them as part of the whole urban nightmare which has increased,
is increasing and ought (by general literary admission) to be

diminished. Third, Burroughs belongs – although that is too precise a term – to the Beat Movement. During the 1950s – after which the Beat, always a loose business, fragmented into variegated clumps of hippies, yippies, flower people, mothers-of-the-earth, recidivist rockers, heads, freaks and the like – beats were *the* drop-outs. It was as if the apparently monochromatic sameness of the period (in instantly nostalgic retrospect we have learned that it was not all the same) allowed the simplest form of opposition. The term 'drop-out' illustrates this. The sameness of society is so 'given' that to drop out is perfectly self-explanatory. Take off, leave, go, abandon – it did not really matter how – but at all costs move at a different rhythm, tune in to another beat, reach for the throb of some more ecstatic pulse. (The Beat Movement need not greatly concern us here; it is one small tile in the very large mosaic of twentieth-century American culture; it has, under the aegis of Allan Ginsberg, a much more enduring influence on American poetry, and its prose manifestations, as in Kerouac and Burroughs, are more significant as a part of some larger entity.)

Burroughs' most accessible book is *Junkie*; reasonably straightforward in shape, it gives a decently conventional view of the life of a drug addict. It is not, however, an especially distinguished book and would, I suspect, have only a sociological interest were it not for the mad intense scramble of his later novels – *The Naked Lunch*, *The Soft Machine*, *Nova Express* and *The Ticket that Exploded*; he has also produced *The Exterminator* in collaboration with Brion Gysin. *The Naked Lunch* is the most representative and, to all but addicts, the most famous of his books, juxtaposing the actual details of a junkie's life with the phantasmagoric distortions in perception that the drugs bring on. Readers who are interested in Burroughs will find a sympathetic treatment in Tony Tanner's *City of Words*; he points out that Burroughs is greatly concerned with the fear of a system taking over from *our* system – that is to say, that drugs are, as it were, an alien occupying force, an evil external power which, once internalised into the human system, transforms and destroys it. This, Tanner correctly suggests, ties in with a prevalent American fear of the corporation, the monopolising bureaucracy, the vast secret service which can unobtrusively enter and destroy the most precious of American commodities – the individuality of the individual. Tanner, again correctly, relates this to the increasing horror of meaninglessness characterised in America by waste and decay. This quality, found in Miller, Burroughs carries to its most extreme point. Nowhere is the pulp side of American life – the world of crumbling tenements, decaying car dumps, poisoned rivers, acres of garbage, cities winding down, a world left carelessly to rot – seen with more disgust.

However, it is difficult to go along with Tanner when, speaking enthusiastically of Burroughs, he says:

> *Naked Lunch* . . . is a book with no narrative continuity, and no sustained point of view; the separate episodes are not inter-related, they co-exist in a particular force brought together by the mind of Burroughs which then abandons them . . . Burroughs describes his book as a blueprint which ranges from insects to planetary landscapes, from abstractions to turds, and this suggests the sort of expansions and contractions of episode which in this book replace linear narrative. And the episodes themselves are experienced as a distribution of fragments rather than as internally organized structures: the most common form of punctuation is simply a row of dots separating image from image, voice from voice, and the book gives us a world beneath or beyond syntax and all that that implies.

That strikes me as one way of saying that *The Naked Lunch* is a very bad book indeed. If the mind of Burroughs manifests itself in so fragmented a way, how are we to recognise this force that brings together episodes in co-existence but not in inter-relationship – a tenuous distinction. A blueprint is traditionally a set of preliminary plans or intentions – a guide which suggests in some coherent way what is to follow; surely a blueprint which accommodated planetary landscapes, insects, turds and abstractions would perforce have to be less not more fragmentary; the connecting signs would have to be stronger. *How* does one experience episodes that are distributed fragments and in what sense can this ever replace narrative, linear or otherwise? Punctuation, let us remember, exists not only to enable us to breathe but to allow our statements the shape and sense we wish for them; thus their substitution by 'simply' a row of dots is to obscure whatever meaning the writer's statements may have; therefore a 'separation' of voice from voice or image from image is just about all we can expect, we cannot hope to clarify what the separation is for. (It is extremely hard to discover in Burroughs when even this 'separation' is taking place; voices and images seem to be part of the same glutinous stew.) And, finally, what exactly is implied by 'a world beneath or beyond syntax'? At best, it suggests that Burroughs deals with a world that is too profound or too fluid to be coped with by language (in which case why use language?). At worst, it implies that the normal coherence of language shows up what Burroughs feels as an inarticulate garbled mess (in which case why turn it into language?). It seems counter-productive.

Burroughs' stress on collage-like devices – the 'cut-out', the 'fold-in', the dissociated scrambling of dreams – is, like his debt to the 'camera eye' sequences in Dos Passos' *USA*, defensive. Cutouts and fold-ins can only work *in a context of their own*, just as Dos Passos' sections do. And the fact is that, although *The Naked Lunch* has moments of circus fun, and moments where slang leaps alive off the page, these remain only moments. The work is incoherent and opaque to a degree which turns any explanation of it into an apology. It does not compare favourably with *Tropic of Cancer* where – even if a sparrow always has to be pecking at a turd – at least we know who is seeing life like that and why. It compares even more unfavourably with the works of Jack Kerouac, and particularly with what became the 'Beat Bible' – his now-classic *On the Road*.

JACK KEROUAC

There was a time when anyone under twenty who had not read *On the Road* was a social leper; and it is natural that the work's trendiness, together with a certain glossy professionalism – as exhibited elsewhere in Kerouac, in *The Dharma Bums*, *Sartori in Paris* and *Maggie Cassidy* – should have turned up a good many high-bridged noses. Some critics see it as the start of all that is worst in 'underground' literature – the commercial posing as the 'free', the advocating as meaningful of a species of adolescent self-indulgence. My own view is that *On the Road* is not only an important book but a good one, and that it is in some respects *the* American mystical novel of the twentieth century.

This book (so autobiographical that some will not allow it to be a novel at all) is narrated by the unambiguously named Sal Paradise; although it contains many characters, it centres on the life and behaviour of his friend, Dean Moriarty – mystic traveller extraordinary, living epitome of Beat. Dean 'is the perfect guy for the road because he actually was born on the road, when his parents were passing through Salt Lake City'. The fact that such a birth is an advantage is immediately significant. Here, at the very beginning of the book, Kerouac is producing a modern revival of the great romantic value of American movement, re-creating the belief that to commune with – that is, to know – his vast country the American must travel it; to be actually born in such movement is to establish unimpeachable mystico-genetic credentials – credentials which are essentially life-giving. Paradise begins the novel with the 'feeling that everything was dead'. Travelling with Dean changes this into the belief that 'somewhere along the line I knew there'd be girls, visions, everything; some-where along the line the pearl would be handed to me. It is easy, out of context, to laugh at such visionary naïveté; but, as it is revealed in and through the character of Dean, it has a lyrical, touching and not altogether unsubtle honesty. For Dean's progress is not only a mystical celebration of the visionary experience of movement (and therefore of certain American qualities) but also of its limitations.

'Dean,' says Paradise, 'had the tremendous energy of a new kind of American saint.' The energy consists in entering everything – especially women – with the wildest possible enthusiasm. The novel ends with him 'three times married, twice divorced, and living with his second wife' – a tangible manifestation of Paradise's belief that, to Dean, sex was 'the one and only holy and important thing in life'. Actually that view (made early in the novel) is modified as we realise that what Dean and Sal seek from life as a whole is the ecstatic and mystical visionary experience they get from sex. The book is therefore full of terms of approbation that suggest experience lifted to an ecstatic level – 'tremendous', 'incredible', 'beautiful', 'wild' and 'ecstatic' itself; and these terms are frequently used in what, at the time, would have been inappropriate situations. A brown paper bag is 'tremendous', not because it is especially large, nor even because it is half-full of groceries for a poor widow, but because at this point Paradise realises what a tremendous thing a brown paper bag can be *if you will only look at it like that*. Kerouac is revealing an imaginative approach oddly similar to Virginia Woolf's; he is discovering and attempting to reveal the wonder of the ordinary, the everyday, the discarded – although Kerouac's discoveries are quintessentially 1950s American. For example, Paradise is given a ride and is left:

> ... at a lonely crossroads on the edge of the prairie. It was beautiful there. The only cars that came by were farmer-cars; they gave one suspicious looks, they clanked along, the cars were coming home. Not a truck. A few cars zipped by. A hotrod kid came by with his scarf flying. The sun went all the way down and I was standing in the purple darkness.

The beauty of the scene is composite of classic American rural/

pastoral (cars, prairie, sunset) with the technological (cars/high-way/cross-roads); the mixture shows especially in the suspicious-ness of the farmers – no pastoral kindness there – which makes Paradise long for a truck. Most telling of all is that it is impossible to imagine that sunset *without the cars*. The Americanness of that scene and the attributes contained in it are shown again and again. Paradise prefers the magic of the names on box-cars, 'Missouri Pacific, Great Northern, Rock Island Line', to the labels on French wine. One of the characters teaches Dean that:

> . . . he can do anything he wants, become mayor of Denver, marry a millionairess, or become the greatest poet since Rimbaud. But he keeps rushing out to see the midget auto races.

Exactly: the midget auto-races, the labels on box-cars, the 'vision' of betting on horses, the shape of gas-stations, the trans-conti-nental presence of pie and ice-cream – all of this is a way of telling Americans of the improbable beauty of their own country; and, in so doing, Kerouac provides a counterpoint to the amazingly brilliant and beautiful journey of Humbert Humbert and Lolita in Nabokov's beautiful and brilliant novel. Kerouac is also antici-pating the great 1960s wave of nostalgia about 1950s style, as seen particularly in the journalism of Tom Wolfe.

One of the novel's subtler points, and indeed one of its best features, consists, as I have said, in Kerouac's communication of the limitations of the characters' mystical sense of experience. The kick which comes from travelling 'four thousand miles from Frisco, via Arizona and up to Denver, inside four days, with in-numerable adventures sandwiched in' is real enough; but where, Kerouac asks, does it take you? As we saw from an earlier quotation, the characters are in pursuit of some extra reality in or through the mystical experience itself – 'the pearl', which is later rephrased simply as 'IT'. They do not get it and the fact that they do not throws into sadly ironic relief the jaunty aggressiveness of statements like 'No matter, the road is life'. Their last trip to

Mexico City reveals to them '. . . the great and final wild un-
hibited Fellahin-childlike city that we knew we would find at the
end of the road'. It reveals also that there *is* an end to the road, a
limit to travelling not only in the physical and emotional sense but
also in the mystical. Because all they find in Mexico City is more of
the same – which still does not produce 'IT'.

Thus, the novel ends on a sad note. Dean's journeying has become frenetic, spasmodic, obsessive. America, asking to be
crossed, again has become 'the awful continent', which offers no
communion that will solve 'the impossible complexity' of Dean's
life, as he shuffles off 'ragged in a motheaten overcoat he bought
specially for the freezing temperatures of the East . . . rounded the
corner of Seventh Avenue, eyes on the street ahead, and bent to
it again'.

The consequences of *On the Road* for popular fiction were not
good. There is a popular song of Carole King's that puts it
aptly:

> Too many songs about moving along the highway
> Can't say much of anything that's new.

And so we get a rash of books with perambulating heroes who,
in their increasing aggressiveness differ unpleasantly from the
joyful Dostoievskian idiot, Dean. One of the better written examples is Richard Fariña's *Been Down So Long It Looks Like Up
To Me*, a novel that enjoyed a brief campus vogue in the late 1960s.
The hero, a literate bum, drifts not as a discoverer but as an
exploiter; although there are attempts to present him as picar-
esquely lovable, he is really a juvenile bastard of a particularly
kitsch kind. His idea of rebellion is to dance on the table during a
fraternity party; his idea of adventure consists in a self-aggrandis-
ing sexual cruelty. His travelling is more like a badge that gains
admittance to the middle-class society he so badly needs to shock
– and which Fariña believes to be easily shockable. Readers who
are quick to dismiss *On the Road* would do well to compare the

pointless nastiness of Fariña's novel with the genial and generous expansiveness of Kerouac.

Readers may be wondering by now whether the distinctions between my original categories of fantasy are valid. Surely Kerouac and Burroughs are just as much social fantasists as mystical ones; surely Miller is greatly concerned with American society? Obviously there *are* grey areas here – as, for instance, Miller seeing the world's sexual problems as partly historico-social. Yet each of these authors is much more concerned with his own experiences – particularly mystical or ecstatic ones – than the society which contributed to their occurrence. Miller describes Paris to show us how *he* feels about it – to give us *his* vision; he doesn't give a damn about French society. Burroughs – who, if anyone should, ought to be delivering some wail about how society produces addicts – concerns himself only with how society is perceived *through* the addict's consciousness, a perception which is concerned much more with the consciousness than the society it observes. Society may be hell bent on waste, but it is the addict's business to cope with it only in so far as it affects him – let society get on with it. And Kerouac, instead of delivering diatribes about the economic hegemony that prevents the perpetual enjoyment of the road's freedom, pays no attention to the subject whatsoever. In contradistinction to post-Kerouac novels (such as Elia Katz's *Armed Love*), *On the Road* does not bother with the reaction of non-bums – or indeed with society's reaction to bums – it stays right there with the beat's own feelings. In their own way, the beats are all as remote as monks – they have their own mystic brotherhood and are content with that.

THE LITERARY FANTASISTS

John Barth, Thomas Pynchon, Richard Brautigan, Donald Barthelme and John Hawkes are all writers producing books about books. My own view is that, except in the case of a very rare talent like Nabokov, this process is escapist – that is to say, it runs away from and manages to keep on avoiding the thing that frightens it, which is the thing it was writing about in the first place. Like the characters in Truman Capote's beautiful and lyrical novel, *The Grass Harp*, these writers, finding the real world painful or inexplicable, go to live in a tree house; but then Capote's characters know what they are doing – one of them, the Judge, says: 'But ah, the energy we spent hiding from one another, afraid as we are of being identified. But here we are, identified: five fools in a tree.' One wonders whether the writers on my list have that degree of self-awareness.

To give two or three examples, beginning with the two writers whom I personally find most over-praised.

Thomas Pynchon and John Hawkes

Pynchon's *V* centres on two characters (although to allow the word 'centre' within barking distance of Pynchon is to distort), Stencil and Benny Profane, who first independently and then jointly become involved in various chaotic episodes in history from the turn of the century to the present day. (The novel is riddled with deliberately weird nomenclature; Pynchon's group of characters living in contemporary America are called 'The Whole Sick Crew' – not without reason.) Throughout the scrambled non-chronology of the novel, throughout its deliberately (I suppose) labyrinthine plot, the characters are in quest of V, a female spy/revolutionary/anarchist who mutates episodically through a series of names and characters always just ahead of the pursuers. Any gloss on the multiple confusions of *V* could run to encyclopaedic length, but it is worth saying that V herself (*is* she Stencil's mother?) turns out to be a 'remarkably scattered concept'; as Tony Tanner points out, if V as a term 'can mean everything it means nothing'.

The world which John Hawkes creates in *The Cannibal* is easier to follow because of his style – in much the same way as a trip through jungle is made quicker by the possession of a sharp knife. He has written several novels, including *The Lime Twig*, *The Beetle Leg* and *Second Skin*, but it is for his first book, *The Cannibal*, that he is best known. This deals principally with the year 1945 and an allied occupation of Germany – '*an* allied' because both the year and the nature of the occupation are treated fantastically. In the Germany of Hawkes's imagination one-third of the country is supervised by a single American on a motorcycle, and the horrors of the real Germany in 1945, which ought to have been horrid enough for anyone, are jacked up several points. As the introduction to the book says –

> ... the tiny gutted Spitzen-on-the-Dein – with its feverish D.P.'s, its diseased impotent adults and crippled children, with its foul choked canals, with its hunger, militarism, primitive memories and its unregenerate hatred of the conqueror – is Germany itself in microcosm. (As a picture of the real rather than the actual Germany, and of the American occupant of that Germany, *The Cannibal* is as frankly distorted as Kafka's picture of the United States in *Amerika*; and also perhaps as true, thanks to that distortion.)

Well now – does distortion necessarily make a thing true? That seems to me a particularly silly modern idea. Distortion has a very valuable part to play in the conveying of truth (literary or otherwise) and its principal role is in forcing people to recognise either something which is obscure or which they do not wish to acknowledge. Neither seems to me to be true of post-war Germany. Hawkes certainly alerts us to both the physical horror of Germany and the psychological horror that made it possible; in the character of Zizendorff, the sadistic leader of a neo-Nazi group, he makes the possibility of a Nazi revival alive enough. So in the circumstances it hardly seems polite to point out that Hawkes was *wrong*. Germany (with the help of a great deal more than one American on a motor-cycle) staged an almost miraculous reconstruction – an achievement which has been straight forwardly positive, and has not led to any significant Nazi revival. Certainly the split between East and West is a nasty problem – but not a nasty Nazi one – and, however much distaste one may feel for the régime in the East, it cannot be accused of the entropic somnolent wastefulness that Hawkes is prophesying. One understands, of course, his position when he published the book in 1949 – a time when Germany could easily have gone under. All I am suggesting is that one cannot claim Hawkes as a successfully prophetic writer any more than one can claim that his distortion forces one to acknowledge the truth. Here the word 'distortion' raises another point. There is, in the human psyche, a capacity for only so much pain. Writers have realised this from the beginning of time – hence the whole notion of relief, comic or otherwise. To provide a world of unrelieved disgust in which the very cat which rubs itself against your leg is inevitably dwarfed, is to offer us something we cannot absorb; human emotions can take only a certain amount of distortion.

This relates to the interesting question of Hawkes's prose. Purists who believe that prose and content always make up a seamless garment should take a look at it. The fact is that Hawkes writes beautifully. His sentences are masterpieces of clarity; his paragraphs are self-propelling rhythmic units. His great superiority over someone like Pynchon is very much a matter of prose. Pynchon's style goes in for a combination of two unsatisfactory elements – modern/orchidaceous and intellectual/camp:

> Dog into wolf, light into twilight, emptiness into waiting presence, here were your underage Marine barking in the street, barmaid and a ship's propeller tattooed on each buttock, one potential berserk studying the best technique for jumping through a plate glass window.

That cannot compete with the purity and clarity of Hawkes –

> Madame Snow hunched over her cards, and the silver platters, goblets and huge bowls grew black with tarnish and thick with

dust. The merciless light showed each house a clear red or flat sand color and long barred beams and ashen barns were black.

It is prose like that which leads the introduction to speak of Hawkes's debt to 'coldly intense writers', and other critics to see him as a classicist – one who by the very balance, coolness, formality of his style makes us realise the ironic force of what it is describing. Yet the coolness in Hawkes divides one from the heat of the content. His is not prose like Swift's or Nathanael West's, in which the detachment is there at a cost, where the author is holding down in the sternest and most disciplined way something that would otherwise overcome him. Rather one comes to enjoy Hawkes's style for its own sake – to escape into the bookishness of the book, to move away from the anguish, which the author is supposedly intending to portray, into the pleasures of the portrayal.

Barthelme, Brautigan and Barth

The problem recurs in the work of this accidentally alliterating trio. In Barthelme's *Snow White*, the fairy tale of the same name is transposed into the modern world, a process which involves a certain amount of jolly incongruity (the seven dwarfs spend a lot of time in the shower with Snow White); the self-conscious, humorously fragmented episodes and the ad-man's trick of using capitalised slogans – PAUL HAS NEVER BEFORE REALLY SEEN SNOW WHITE AS A WOMAN' – give the book a cheerful op-art look. The reader is invited both to participate in the creation of the book and to admire the result – with the consequence that, whatever Barthelme's content may be (and the book is a hotchpotch of wise-cracks about ideologies, sex, violence and death), it becomes merely a part of an agreeable literary game.

The same point applies – though perhaps less obviously – to the works of the talented Richard Brautigan. His titles give the game away: *In Watermelon Sugar* and *A Confederate General from Big*

Sur are both obviously ironic, while *Trout Fishing in America* is totally tongue-in-cheek. This last-named makes a skilful and amusing use of many of Barthelme's techniques plus the liberal use of lists, diaries, confessions and any other verbal paraphernalia that may fall to hand. The advantage Brautigan has over Barthelme is that his incidents are all strung on the same thematic thread – the author's attempt to find some decent trout fishing and, on his failure, the realisation of America's ecological and therefore moral decline. Brautigan has a lively as well as a vivid imagination which seems naturally at home in a world of zany and self-consciously literary movement. Although, in ecology, Brautigan handles a subject sociologically immediate to the point of being trendy, there is never a moment when his book does not draw attention to itself; his continual personifying of trout fishing is always amusing but it is always more striking by its ingenuity than by its justness.

> Trout Fishing in America Shorty appeared suddenly last autumn in San Francisco, staggering around in a magnificent chrome-plated steel wheelchair. He was a legless, screaming middle-aged wino ... He would stop children on the street and say to them, 'I ain't got no legs. The trout chopped my legs off in Fort Lauderdale. You kids got legs. The trout didn't chop your legs off. Wheel me into that store over there.'
> The kids frightened and embarrassed, would wheel Trout Fishing in America Shorty into the store ...

Trout Fishing in America Shorty is very funny and as an idea has a touch of the pleasantly light macabre. But what are we to make of him? Is he supposed to illustrate the pillaging redneck hunter who destroys trout fishing? What are we to make of the trout cutting off his legs? It's funny all right, but what does it mean? Is the reaction of the children meant to suggest society's embarrassed reaction to the pollution of the environment – or are we intended to see that Shorty is the substitute for nature left to the American young? The answer lies in Shorty's reappearance:

Last week, 'The New Wave' took him out of his wheelchair and laid him out in a cobblestone alley. Then they shot some footage of him. He ranted and raved and they put it down on film.

Later on, probably, a different voice will be dubbed in. It will be a noble and eloquent voice denouncing man's inhumanity to man in no uncertain terms.

'Trout Fishing in America Shorty, Mon Amour'.

In fact, Brautigan is 'hanging loose' – he is really in business for the fun of it; the point there is not that we think for a moment about the media exploitation of ecological questions; the point is the pleasure we get from the joke and the pleasure Brautigan gets from our pleasure. The book has other elements which confirm this impression. There is a good deal of *kitsch* whimsy in the style:

> The fall had not appreciably helped the thickness of the cat, and then a few people had parked their cars on the cat. Of course, that was a long time ago and the cars looked different from the way they look now.

– which does not really work in a book so variously pregnant with meanings: 'I saw a dead fish come forward and float into my sperm, bending it in the middle. His eyes were stiff like iron.' The last word of the book is 'mayonnaise'.

In Barth we encounter a more difficult example of the same case. With the exception of Pynchon (than whom nobody could be more pretentious), he makes much larger claims than the other literary fantasists. His two major works – *The Sot Weed Factor* and *Giles Goat-Boy* – are novels of mammoth length affording some readers limitless joy and others endless aggravation. They are both academic books (Barth is a college professor) and, in their creation of an essentially scholarly fantasy world, the influence of Nabokov is sometimes detected. In *The Sot Weed Factor*, Barth produces what has frequently been called a 'spoof' on American history – and the vital question is whether it stays on the spoof level. The novel is mock-historic, centring on the Early American Experiences of a lost innocent, Ebenezer Cooke, who did in fact exist and who did in reality produce a poem called 'The Sot-Weed Factor' in 1708. The book is long, strange and tries very hard to be funny, its principal humorous source being scatology, and its final aim to turn American – and to some extent European – history on its head. Thus the onward progress of America – apportioned in so much official literary and historical legend to the clean-limbed, the fresh-eyed, the independent – is here entrusted to the dubiously wily *picaro*, Burlingame, whose fictional conduct Barth uses to rewrite tender American myths. Barth clearly took great care and pleasure in the book's construction; it is full of historical detail, much of it apparently discovered in the Archives of Maryland, and he has fun with America on every page. But once again we meet the question: is fun really all he is having? Readers will, of course, decide for themselves.

In the later *Giles Goat-Boy*, their decision will be no easier. It is crammed with literary references – some familiar, some obscure – starting off from a bewildering introduction composed of a series of letters (publishers' readers' letters, author's cover letter, etc) which throw a series of doubts on the author and his intention. The world here is a confused and confusing university in which a bewildering series of characters compete bewilderingly over tasty little nuggets, like 'truth'. Even if the reader does not feel as I do about Barth – that he is too long and too childishly coarse – and even if *Giles Goat-Boy* is saying a series of important and complex things, there is still the question of why Barth chooses to present them in this way. For his fantasy has only nebulous connections with any one of our many realities; what we ultimately come away with is the bookishness of the book.

Readers will have gathered by now that I am not over-fond of the literary fantasists; they will also have gathered, by the periodic eruption of his name, that I consider Nabokov to be of them but above them. Before I go into that, however, I should say a few brief words about what I have termed the 'social fantasists'.

These, although they work in various degrees of fantasy, primarily look not inward to the book but outward to society, which is still for them a real concern.

THE SOCIAL FANTASISTS

Four prominent ones come to mind: Vonnegut, Heller and Kesey and – in a sense the daddy of them all – Nathanael West. Of these, Vonnegut receives a wider hearing under 'Science Fiction' (page 185) and West under 'The Jewish-American Novel' (page 162). We are left then with Joseph Heller and Ken Kesey who, respectively in *Catch-22* and *One Flew Over the Cuckoo's Nest*, have provided us with something interesting and valuable. Because *Catch-22* is better known and has received more – perhaps too much – comment, I shall concentrate on *One Flew Over the Cuckoo's Nest*. Like *On the Road*, it suffers from being a campus cult novel. Although the book itself has very little to do with drugs, its author certainly had. Kesey was the centre of a group experimenting elaborately and publicly with LSD (wittily examined by Tom Wolfe in *The Electric Kool-Aid Acid Test*) and that fact alone was enough to lend to the book's supposed attack on the American Establishment a notoriety it does not possess. The book in fact attacks things in American society rather than the entire society itself, and in so doing makes a very skilful use of fantasy.

The novel is set in a lunatic asylum and narrated by a gigantic and virtually schizophrenic Red Indian chief. His ward in the asylum is ruled over by a monster of sweetness, light and unmitigated power-lust, known as the Big Nurse. She and her trio of cruel – and themselves disturbed – black helpers have reduced the patients to a state of abject subservience. A combination of the petty (ridiculous rules and small persecutions) and the great (electric-shock treatment, lobotomy) keeps the patients as Big Nurse's toys. Into this scene explodes McMurphy, a powerful Irish American who has got himself transferred to the asylum to escape from the hard life of a prison farm. The substance of the book is the enthralling battle between McMurphy and Big Nurse for control of the ward.

On one level this is a straightforward struggle between good and evil. Aggressively masculine and formidably independent, McMurphy tries by a number of devices (the most colourful being the introduction of prostitutes into the ward) to re-establish the masculinity and the individuality of which Big Nurse is robbing the men. On another level we are dealing with a struggle central to the whole of American society, and it is here that fantasy comes in. For, to the Red Indian chief, the ward is in the grip of an alien impersonal corporate power which he calls the Combine: 'The ward is a factory for the Combine. It's for fixing up mistakes made in the neighbourhoods and in the schools and in the churches.' He imagines a long list of almost science-fiction horrors to which the patients are subjected by the Combine. One of the simplest is a machine that pumps fog over the patient's mind; while the most outrageous envisages the whole ward wired to bizarrely complicated specifications, so that at night the floors slip down into the bowels of the earth where the Combine's workers overhaul patients like machines.

> The worker takes the scalpel and slices up the front of old Blastic with a clean swing, and the old man stops thrashing around. I expect to be sick, but there's no blood or innards falling out like I was going to see – just a shower of rust and ashes, and now again a piece of wire or glass.

One of the novel's best features is the way in which we have to pick our way through the chief's fantasies, not sure how true any of them are. With the chief we are in a state of horrific uncertainty; this, like the fog, clears as the story progresses and McMurphy does his work. The end of the novel, the point at which so many of the patients rejoin society, is also the point where all the fantasies are finally cleared away, and actual horror and actual joy can be distinguished from their phantasmagoric equivalents. Thus there *is* a form of mechanistic corporate horror in the asylum – electric-shock treatment and lobotomies do happen – and this *is* an analogue of society, or at any rate of an element within it.

Kesey has always been keen on cartoons. More than one critic has seen evidence of this in *One Flew Over the Cuckoo's Nest*, finding a possibly damaging cartoon simplicity in the characters. McMurphy is continually being described as a cowboy (he actually imitates cowboy speech and, prior to any confrontation, he goes through the thumbs-in-belt, trouser-hitching, gallus-snapping ritual of the Western gunfighter under pressure). Big Nurse is called by that cartoon-sounding nickname so often that it is a surprise to hear her referred to as Miss Ratchett (McMurphy uses her real name as a special goad), while the chief is like an animated drug-store Indian, a stereotyped symbol of enslaved strength. While some critics dislike this, others admire what they see as Kesey's adaptation of genuinely simple American myths. The chief says of McMurphy:

> Maybe . . . the Combine missed getting to him soon enough with controls. Maybe he growed up all over the country, batting around from one place to another, never around one town longer'n a few months when he was a kid so a school never got much a hold on him, logging, gambling, running carnival wheels, traveling light-footed and fast.

The language is the familiar slang that comes out of mouths in balloons; the content, Huck Finn in pictures.

Yet to leave things like that is to leave them too simply. First, if one had never read a comic paper or seen a cartoon, it would not damage one's enjoyment of the book – which suggests that the cartoon element is not greatly pronounced; secondly, the movement of both character and plot is out of stereotype into complexity. All the characters, particularly the chief and McMurphy, start off seeing events in comic-book terms: THERE IS A NIGHT-

MARE SYSTEM – GEE WELL WE'VE GOTTA FACE IT DOWN, but discover that life is not so simple.

After apparently defeating Big Nurse, McMurphy learns that, unlike most of the other inmates, he has been committed; he can be discharged only by his enemy's good offices. He then finds he can't just play at being a good boy to win his release; he has created a resistance in the others that needs his help, and the giving of the help that saves them destroys him. When the others have achieved freedom it is McMurphy who is left, a lobotomised vegetable fit only for mercy killing at the hands of the chief.

If any further evidence of the novel's complexifying were needed, we should point to the irony involved as, waiting for his first bout of electric-shock treatment, McMurphy goes into the old routine:

> 'McMurphy's the name, pardners,' he said in his drawling cowboy actor's voice, 'and the thing I want to *know* is who's the pecker-wood runs the poker game in this establishment?'

McMurphy knows this is not something that can be faced down – events and reactions have grown too complex for that; yet, in holding to the old way, he asserts his belief in the very individuality that the machine will eventually destroy. The movement from cartoon stereotype to human being is complete.

The social fantasist thus establishes or explores the relationship between fantasy and reality by moving through one to the other, or at any rate attempting to, for the quest is not always successful. In Vonnegut's *Slaughterhouse Five*, in Norman Mailer's *Barbary Shore*, in Joseph Heller's *Catch-22*, the distinction between the fantastic and the real is at best only teeteringly preserved. Towards the end of Heller's novel the hero, Yossarian, takes a walk through an Italian city's slums, and finds there an absolute confirmation of what he had only been able to half-convince himself up till now – that it is the world that is crazy, not him. Again, what we have here is the character's advance through a fantastically perceived world (Majors promoted by IBM computers with a keen sense of humour; Milo Minderbinder, mad wheeler-dealer virtually selling the American army to the enemy; Arfy, the murdering vegetable) into whatever it is about the fantasy that is real. This is, I suggest, the important area where the social and literary fantasists differ: the social fantasist wishes to see how far what would commonly be considered fantasy is now reality, how far nightmares are true and how in the face of their truth man should act. The literary fantasist who has found it all too much for him has decided that the only possible area of freedom is within the form he has created, he has given up worrying about what is real and what fantastic – which process is the beginning of living wholly in fantasy.

VLADIMIR NABOKOV

This is the point to introduce Nabokov; like other great writers before him, he is able to transcend categories and limitations, and his movement from reality through fantasy and back again is little short of sublime. First, however, we ought to clear up the question of his literary citizenship. Born a Russian aristocrat, educated at Cambridge, he lived in Germany and France, emigrated to America, then moved to Switzerland where he paid American income tax – where are we to put Nabokov? The question takes on even more frenetic life when we learn that he wrote a number of distinguished novels in Russian before he turned to English.

> My private tragedy, which cannot, and indeed should not, be anybody's concern, is that I had to abandon my natural idiom, my untrammelled, rich, and infinitely docile Russian tongue for a second-rate brand of English, devoid of any of those apparatuses – the baffling mirror, the black velvet backdrop, the implied associations and traditions – which the native illusionist, frac-tails flying, can magically use to transcend the heritage in his own way.

133

Whatever Nabokov intended by this, and whatever the merits of his Russian, any suggestion that his English is second-rate should be taken not with a pinch but with a whole cellar of salt. For in Nabokov we are confronted with the most acute modern paradox – that one of the greatest masters of the English language lived in exile from another tongue. Yet Nabokov must be judged as an American writer, not merely because of his American citizenship – which he took seriously – but because in at least three of his novels (*Lolita*, *Pale Fire* and *Ada*) he commemorates and celebrates America with a beauty and an understanding that is the greatest of personal tributes. 'Mais j'adore l'Amerique,' he said, when confronted by the vulgar suggestion that *Lolita* is anti-American – and he did.

That fantasy and illusion were important to Nabokov can be seen in the above quotation. Even if he regretted the absence of Russian 'apparatuses', he certainly made ample use (some would say too much) in his English novels of the arts of the illusionist. Yet, as we can see in his incredible *Pale Fire*, these arts transcend their own apparent limitations.

Pale Fire consists of three sections: an introduction to a poem entitled 'Pale Fire', the poem itself, followed by a commentary on its text. The poem is supposedly written by an American, John Shade, the rest supposedly by one Charles X. Kinbote. I say 'supposedly' because, as the 'novel' unfolds through the relationship between the three structural divisions, doubts multiply. Kinbote who, like Shade, lived near and taught at the small New England college of Wordsmith, claims to be living in retreat to escape from Shade's widow and her cohorts who want to stop him from editing the poem. No wonder, for the notes are 5 per cent about the text, 25 per cent about Shade and 70 per cent about Kinbote. He (Kinbote) claims to be the exiled king of a 'distant Northern', gently Ruritanical country called Zembla, recently overrun by revolution. Kinbote does everything in his power to twist the poem away from its actual subjects (life, love and the hereafter, with special reference to the suicide of Shade's daughter) and read into it his own history – an irony there, since the bumblingly idiotic assassin, Gradus, shoots Shade instead of Kinbote. (It is amusing that one of the most 'fantastic' elements of the plot should be based on the hardest of facts: Nabokov's own father was assassinated by mistake.)

As if the poem/notes' conflict was not puzzling enough, we soon learn that the book is full of gleeful snags. Kinbote is only tenuously sane – how much of what he says are we to believe? Is 'Pale Fire', and therefore the poet Shade, Kinbote's creation; or could it be the other way round – the whole thing a Shadean game? There are clues in these, and other, directions; one critic has remarked that, like the image of the bird in the poem 'Pale Fire',

> I was the shadow of the waxwing slain
> By feigned remoteness in the windowpane

the reader meets in Nabokov's work mirrors where he expects windows. Other critics who dislike the whole process, who feel his cleverness to be narcissistic gamesmanship, find that there is altogether too much 'feigning' about the work. The issue is too large and live to be debated here, but it is worth saying something about the book's last page, where Kinbote, having completed his 'edition', discusses what he may do next. His list is one of many disguises, many possibilities:

> I may pander to the simple tastes of theatrical critics and cook up a stage play, an old-fashioned melodrama with three principles: a lunatic who intends to kill an imaginary king, another lunatic who imagines himself to be that king, and a distinguished old poet who stumbles by chance into the line of fire, and perishes in the clash between the two figments ... But whatever happens, wherever the scene is laid, somebody, somewhere will quietly set out – somebody has already set out, somebody still rather further away is buying a ticket, is boarding a bus, a ship, a plane, has landed, is walking toward a million photographers, and presently he will

ring at my door – a bigger, more respectable, more competent Gradus.

There are a variety of ways of responding to that, but two main ones emerge: either the king is joking with the reader about his (the king's) capacity for disguise, about the doubts and puzzles he has made for the reader, or, on the other hand, Kinbote is recognising his own lunacy. But whether we accept neither of these positions, or one of them, the final comments about a new and final Gradus are important. For surely in that last sentence Nabokov wishes us to accept that, whatever it is Gradus may represent, that thing is real and ominous for our character, be he king, Kinbote or the Shade that embraces them both. Something real is coming – keepers for Kinbote, assassins for king, death for rheumatic-hearted Shade. And that is beautifully in keeping with the novel, for whatever fantasy is being played out, one clear and unmistakable fact keeps emerging – the fact of the central figure's emotions – his pure mad joy at things, his suffering, his existence as – however demented – an individual. This is the relationship between fantasy and reality in a good Nabokov novel; the fantasy deals with real people. Just at the moment when the beautiful web of illusion seems at its most self-referential, something from a real individual shows through. Thus it is that Nabokov shimmies past the cage door waiting open for other literary fantasists. This argument can be applied even more forcefully to Nabokov's famous novel *Lolita*. Before discussing it I must make an apology. All Nabokov's novels are complex, and complex in a way that makes a proper discussion of them dependent on exegesis of a lengthy kind which this book cannot accommodate. I raise this point so that the reader should not be misled by the comparatively brief space accorded him – and I raise it the more forcefully since the upholder of Nabokov's claims to greatness as a novelist still finds himself in a defensive position. Of course there are elements in the whole Nabokov *oeuvre* about which even the adoring reader may feel some reservation – his authorial omnipotence sometimes signals a terrified sense of superiority that is acceptable only when it cracks; there is a willingness in him to talk down to God Himself; the perversity of his tricks can be carried to sadistically elaborate lengths; it has been suggested that he has a special love for neglected things, but *only* neglected things. Nabokov has faults – no writer is without them; but to concentrate on these at the expense of his manifold talents is as inaccurate as to suppose that these same faults damage all of his books equally. It is high time that what Nabokov gives us should receive as much attention as what he supposedly withholds.

I want to make only one point about *Lolita*, this beautifully complex book, though it is a point which makes its beauty and complexity more striking. I refer to the relationship between social and literary fantasy; because here Nabokov reverses what are problems for other writers, and turns them into advantages. Where other writers are trapped in a no-go area of their own devising, in which literary fantasy and literal reality are hopelessly confused, Nabokov creates a country of the imagination in which reality continually leads us into fantasy and vice-versa, a country in short where fantasy and reality have a proper relationship; and along the way he pulls off another achievement – by deliberately portraying American society through the bizarre eye of Humbert Humbert, he gives us what surely must be one of the most realistic portrayals of America ever.

The whole of *Lolita* is one long illustration of this; but let us consider only one example – the character of Quilty, Humbert's rival, the eventual stealer-away of Lolita. When Humbert finally tracks Lolita down and she tells him what Nabokov describes mockingly as 'the name that the astute reader has guessed long ago', there must be a mass of readers who, like Humbert himself, had no idea that the name was Quilty, yet who immediately connect a number of references stretching back to the Foreword. Nabokov continually invites us to think of Quilty as Humbert's *doppelgänger*, and certainly, wherever Humbert is, there, tracking, trailing, half-hidden in the shadows of Nabokov's plot is Quilty, parodying Humbert's life. While this process is puzzling and interesting and stimulating, it has its problems. For it does begin to seem as if Nabokov is whimsically engaging in the self-referential narcissistic literary in-joke so dangerously common to modern fantasists; the half-revelation of Quilty's name and presence are there, critics suggest, to remind the reader that this is a clever book by a clever author – a game in which he is both sides and the umpire, while we are the ball. This impression would seem to be supported by the large quantity of literary references that stare up at us from every page. Is Nabokov, particularly in his use of Quilty, not being trivially flippant about something that ought, given Humbert's self-torturings, to be serious?

> We fell to wrestling again. We rolled over the floor, in each other's arms, like two huge helpless children. He was naked and goatish under his robe and I felt suffocated as he rolled over me. I rolled over him. We rolled over me. They rolled over him. We rolled over us.

That is, as Nabokov spells out in the next paragraph, an amusing parody of the 'obligatory' Western fight sequence which has become the ridiculously 'silent, soft, formless tussle on the part of two literati, one of whom was utterly disorganised by a drug while the other was handicapped by a heart condition and too much gin'. Yet we also have the puzzling culmination of the *doppelgänger* theme in the deliberate merging of Humbert and Quilty – 'we rolled over us'. We know that Quilty is a sort of horrifying parody of Humbert; Quilty's perversion, his tracking down and stealing of Lolita, and his predisposition towards games, both living and literary, are all exaggeratedly nasty and heartless versions of Humbert's own character. Is not this final description of them together a sign of Nabokov's excessively artful gamesmanship? For, after all, *is* there a relationship between Quilty and Humbert? Is one of the characters perhaps a figment of the other's imagination? If so, which? And is not the only reality to be found that we are all, characters and readers alike, Nabokov's playthings?

This argument overlooks one of Nabokov's most exceptional gifts, which is not for parody but for parodying parody. He mocks, but ultimately he mocks his own mockery. When he describes Humbert and Quilty rolling over together like one person, he is not only continuing the *doppelgänger* idea which sees Quilty as a parody of Humbert but, parodying, has cauterised it. How ridiculous, he in effect says, that reality is so like one's parody of it! It is this cancelling out of parody by parody that makes the great climactic moments of *Lolita* so moving. As, for example, when Lolita – aged, bespectacled, married and pregnant – refuses to go away with the sobbing Humbert:

> 'No,' she said. 'No, honey, no.'
> She had never called me honey before.

The few straightforward moments like that succeed partly because their authenticity is, as it were, guaranteed by their surroundings. Parody and the parody of parody have cauterised every possible cliché and triteness, cheapness and sentimentality from a situation that could so easily be riddled with all of them. Humbert and Lolita have never really spoken to each other before; their communication has always been distorted by Humbert's perversion, and there is always a danger that such moments of breakthrough will fall flat. Here, however, all the fantasies of Humbert's consciousness, all the phantasmagoria of his weird inverted world lead eventually to something as real as rock.

Lolita's use of 'honey' there brings me to a postscript on Nabokov and society. Nabokov always despised 'messages', social or otherwise, and persistently attacked attempts to inject 'meaning' into art, and he had scant sympathy with writers who want to grind social axes on literature's anvil. Yet, if he had nothing to 'say' about America, he had everything to tell. Charlotte Haze, in *Lolita*, 'purchasing new shades and new blinds, returning them to the store, replacing them by others, and so on, in a constant chiaroscuro of smiles and frowns, doubts and pouts', is only one small illustration of the vulgar/genteel fantasies of American advertising that haunt the novel. And the beauty of *Lolita* in this regard is not only that it describes so much of America – roads, motels, small towns, kids, slang – so perfectly, so memorably and so briefly, but also that it captures the rhythms, the movements, the very feeling of American life.

CHAPTER 4

The Minorities
Black Fiction The Jewish-American Novel

The term 'minority' is relatively new. Once, if he were trying to be polite, the 'pure' American would talk of 'people' or 'communities' – the Negro people, the black community; it is, therefore, a measure of the alteration in attitudes that 'minority' should have become a live word suggesting as it does the relationship of a part to a whole, rather than something alien which had strayed accidentally into the midst of an unwilling society. It is also a term rich in social implications, for not all minorities are racial; the growth of minority-consciousness has given use to a plethora of groups demanding social recognition. Ten years from now any introduction to minority fiction will almost certainly have far more novels to consider concerning the role of homosexuals in society, and the liberation of women – who constitute a minority in all but the numerical senses. The sociology of women's liberation is currently well ahead of its literature; among a number of interesting women novelists, only Joan Didion, in her *Play it as it Lays*, and Cynthia Buchanan, with her admirable first novel, *Maiden* (and possibly Mary Macarthy in *The Company She Keeps*), deliberately portray exploited women with real literary force. In time, if the prophets of gloom are correct, we may even confront the paradox of individuals as a separate minority, for modern literature increasingly shows them as a vanishing species systematically hunted to death by the mass.

BLACK FICTION

American Negroes must surely – with the exception of the Jews – possess the invidious distinction of providing the most virulent long-term illustration of majority abuse – an abuse which was literary as well as social. White writers have not notably succeeded in portraying black experience; there are only a few main exceptions to this.

The fin-de-siècle novelist, Kate Chopin, produced a sensitive treatment of miscegenation in her story 'Desirée's Baby' (from her collection *Bayou Folk*), though this concerns having a drop of Negro blood rather than being a Negro. The first half-way successful attempt to portray Negro consciousness comes, oddly enough, from Gertrude Stein (famous otherwise for lesbianism and the pre-Hemingwayan opacity of her style); 'Melanctha', one of the stories from her *Three Lives*, deals graphically with the daughter of a mulatto mother and a Negro father, and anticipates the terrified racial guilt of Faulkner's *Light in August* and *Absalom, Absalom!*. Yet these are the exception rather than the rule. Too much white writing about blacks continued to show the influence of Harriet Beecher Stowe's *Uncle Tom's Cabin* (described by J. C. Furnas as a 'well-meaning, delicately vulgar, subtly tainted piece of cultural subversion') whose racial stereotypes of the Negro as a soulful, artistic, *charming* adjunct to white society live on to dominate such novels as Carl Van Vechten's *Nigger Heaven*. The other turn which the white novelist takes is exemplified by William Styron's *The Confessions of Nat Turner* – a decent attempt to give an account of the psychological deprivation that comes from and is passed down by slavery, it fails by its very decency; the whole is too enthusiastic an assumption of white guilt, and it is too much a novel of the *white* conscience.

To find the black experience well portrayed we must turn to black writers themselves. Apart from the steadily increasing number of lesser-known writers (John Williams, Charles Wright, Chester Himes, Cyrus Colter, William Melvin Kelly, Ishmael Reed) there are, of course, three most prominent novelists – Richard Wright, James Baldwin and Ralph Ellison.

Richard Wright
Historically, Wright takes precedence – his classic *Native Son* being seen as the first black American novel of real stature. It is divided into three appropriately entitled sections – Fear, Flight and Fate – each measuring the stages of the hero, Biggar Thomas, on his journey from a rat-infested Chicago slum to the electric chair. Fear is what Biggar is born to; flight what he is driven to, and fate that he must be destroyed.

> 'Goddammit look! We live here and they live there. We black and they white. They get things and we can't. It's just like living in jail. Half the time I feel like I'm on the outside of the world peeping in through a knothole in the fence.'

This early outburst from Biggar turns out to be deeply significant; when he is on trial for murder, the lawyer pleading for Biggar's life makes the bitterly true point:

> [that prison] holds advantages for him that a life of freedom never had. . . . You could be for the first time conferring *life* upon him. He would be brought for the first time within the orbit of our civilisation. He would have an identity, even though it be but a number. He would have for the first time an openly designated relationship with the world. The very building . . . would be the best he had ever known. Sending him to prison would be the first recognition of his personality he has ever had.

There is no better indictment of the conditions in which Biggar has been raised; no better indication of the intolerable frustrating depersonalisation of colour prejudice, and no clearer indication of the appeal that Wright is making to the reader, like Biggar's lawyer, to *realise* what it is like to be Biggar. It is in conveying this realisation, in compelling us to look and go on looking whether we want to or not, that Wright takes us beneath sociological details to emotional truth. The ironic circumstances of Biggar's murders show this. He is given what is for a Negro the biggest chance imaginable – the job of chauffeur to a liberal white millionaire, Dalton, a philanthropist who believes in sending 'suitable' Negroes to college. Dalton's daughter Mary, involved with a communist group, carries principles into practice by treating the discomfited and terrified Biggar as altogether too much of a human being. After a nightmarishly egalitarian ride, Biggar finishes up in the drunken Mary's bedroom; her blind mother comes in and Biggar, terrified that Mary will reveal his presence, attempts to silence the girl but accidentally smothers her with a pillow. He goes on to kill his girl-friend Bessie (he is afraid she will betray him), thus presenting, when he is caught, a picture of the utmost callousness that confirms the worst white prejudices about the unreformable and inhuman animality of the Negro. Amongst other things, he is wrongly accused of raping Mary, a thought which gives press and public a particularly prurient pleasure.

There are many good features to Wright's novel (not least the style, which – like Baldwin's after him – is strong, graceful and natural), chief among them being his ability to convey the subtleties of the social situation – subtleties that later come to be realised as fundamental to black/white relations. First, the ghetto Negro has little opportunity to use his anger and frustration, to establish his manhood, *except* through crime. He can either accept the guilt for being alive which the white man thrusts on him (when Biggar's family visits him in jail he feels they 'might be glad' because he has taken on the sin of being black that they always accepted) or he can break free.

'. . . I ain't worried none about them women I killed. For a little while I was free. I was doing something. It was wrong, but I was feeling all right . . . I killed 'em cause I was scared and mad. But I been scared and mad all my life and after I killed that first woman, I wasn't scared no more for a little while.'

Here Wright touches on a theme that recurs in so many of the best works of black non-fiction (Claude Brown's *Manchild in the Promised Land* and *The Autobiography of Malcolm X* are two prominent examples) – namely, that in a situation of oppression only the Negro criminal can be unoppressed; he alone steps outside the society's prevailing conditions, he alone asserts his manhood. Hence the irony of the slang term 'bad nigger' which to the racist white is one of disapprobation and to the Negro community one of awed respect. Thus we understand Biggar when he says, in the novel's last pages: '. . . I didn't know I was really alive in this world until I felt things hard enough to kill for 'em.'

Only in death can the Negro find life. *Native Son* also contains a neat condemnation of what was known then as the white liberal conscience. Dalton, Biggar's employer, dispenses what Wright depicts as a largely irrelevant charity. He 'forgives' Biggar for the murder and, professing his goodwill towards Negroes, despatches ping-pong tables to boys' clubs, simultaneously ignoring the fact that he is a slum landlord and that the conditions in which Biggar was raised were as much his fault as anyone's. What this amounts to is that self-justifying philanthropy is not much better than out-and-out bigotry and the net result is that there is a big explosion coming.

The feeling of resentment and the balked longing for some kind of fulfilment and exultation . . . stalk . . . through the land. The consciousness of Biggar Thomas and millions of others more or less like him, white and black, according to the weight of the pressure we have put upon them, forms the quicksands upon which the foundations of our civilization rest. Who knows when some slight shock, disturbing the delicate balance between social order and thirsty aspiration shall send the skyscrapers in our cities toppling?

The words belong to Max, Biggar's defence lawyer, as he sums up at the trial; they stress another important theme in black literature – that white future is now bound up in black future, that however much each may want to segregate (for Negroes can be separatist too), it is not feasible.

At this point we might say a word about Marxism. The only white people who try to help Biggar are Marxists: murdered Mary, her boy-friend Jan, the lawyer Max. And they are not utterly unsuccessful.

> [Biggar] was hugging the proud thought that Max had made the speech all for him, to save his life. It was not the meaning of the speech that gave him pride, but the mere act of it. That in itself was something.

Yet Wright's attitude to Marxism is paradoxical. It is not clear to what extent Max understands Biggar nor how far the social upheaval posed by Marxism can provide a solution to Negro problems; and it is not clear whether Biggar is reacting to Max as a Marxist or just as a white man. This is one of the many issues raised in *Native Son* which receive a more thorough treatment in what is without doubt *the* black American novel of the twentieth century – Ralph Ellison's *Invisible Man*.

Ralph Ellison

This spectacular novel centres on the ambiguity of the black American's position or, to be more exact, his positions. Consider the unfortunate Trueblood, sleeping in a tiny cabin between wife and daughter, and waking from a dream to find himself committing incest.

> '. . . I can't move 'cause I figgers if I moved it would be a sin. And I figgers too, that if I don't move it maybe ain't no sin . . . But once a man gets himself in a tight spot like that it ain't up to him no longer. There I was tryin' to git away with all my might, yet having

to move *without* movin'. I done thought 'bout it since a heap, and when you think right hard you see that's the way things is always been with me.'

Trueblood's position is dreadfully ironic; clearly Ellison wishes to take the last sentence as indicative of the condition of the Negro in America. Society drives the Negro into positions where whatever he does is wrong, yet he must still *do something*; the result a frenzied tension. This theme is picked up several times; early n, the hero and other black boys stage an appalling species of adiatorial combat for a convention of white businessmen. efore their boxing match, a white stripper performs and the retched black adolescents are forced into an especially am-iguous position – inculcated with the knowledge that lusting for white woman is suicidal, they don't know whether to look or ot; yet the whites present are urging them on, some telling them look, others threatening them if they do. They are caught in the ilemma of not knowing which white myth they should be em-odying – that of Negro subservience or that of fathomless black ist for white flesh. Again the result is to produce an almost hizophrenic tension – a tension which underlines the impossi-ility of individual choice or action. The Negro's behaviour is ready predetermined and a situation, which would be difficult iough for any adolescent, is rendered impossible. Yet it is this ate of impossibility which white society perpetuates and re-ards. Trueblood's very name illustrates this; he is, genetically eaking, all that white society expects from the Negro: the ommitter of incest, the passer-on of tainted blood, the *animal*. He so bears the white man's guilt for him. He tells his story to the hite liberal millionaire, Norton, who has incestuous feelings for is own daughter – feelings he lets Trueblood act through for im. The result is that Trueblood gets a hundred-dollar bill for lustrating the basic ambiguity of the black's position – that he in achieve recognition only by identifying with and indeed king responsibility for white fantasies.

The hero's course in *Invisible Man* is one long brilliant illustration of this, and one long search for a solution. The hero, who significantly is never named – but who is significantly 'given' various names by the groups he encounters – attempts to find himself by identifying with a number of different groups or movements. He tries first to be the white liberals' idea of the educated Negro, who while 'knowing his place' is able to 'raise' his 'race', but is expelled from his college for showing the aforesaid Norton what he *asks* to see rather than what he *wants* to see. In the process the hero discovers the duplicity of black collaboration; Bledsoe, the president of his college, thrives on total hypocrisy:

'I's big and black and I say "Yes suh" as loudly as any burr-head when it's convenient, but I'm still the king down here. I don't care how much it appears otherwise ... I've made my place ... and I'll have every Negro in the country hanging on tree limbs by morning if it means staying where I am.'

The reference to hangings puts Bledsoe on the same level as the Southern racist; he thinks of the Negro in the same way, and will take the same steps to maintain the *status quo*.

The fact is that, wherever the hero turns, the situation is impossible; wherever he goes, like Trueblood, he cannot move but he also cannot *not* move. He goes to work in a paint factory where he becomes sandwiched between the dreadful alternatives of the mad Lucas Brockway and the apparently equally mad trade union. In the creation of Brockway, Ellison reaches a Dickensian combination of humour, horror and symbolic force. The whole paint plant ultimately depends on the paranoid, cellar-dwelling Brockway, who alone can mix the colour 'optic white' which everyone wants. The significance of the colour-name is self-evident, but equally important is Brockway's own definition of his role: 'They got all this machinery, but that ain't everything; *we are the machines inside the machine.*'

In other words, without the Brockways of this world American society would not go on; 'we', as Brockway says, 'make the best white paint in the world' – black people run a society for white people in which blacks are continually subservient, and this is a position of which characters like Brockway are not only proud but are afraid of losing. At a time when others are rebelling against the mechanism of American society, Brockway, like so many Negroes, wants to belong at any price, even if it means being a machine.

The Invisible Man who will not be content with the monstrous unreality of the situation encounters three possible solutions. The first is the Brotherhood, a multi-racial Marxist group which discovers the hero's talents as an orator, teaches him that the Negro's vicissitudes are part of a wider class struggle, and ultimately exploits him; they crown their narrow-minded sloganising by deciding that it would be momentarily expedient to have a riot in Harlem – the black has moved from being part of a struggle to being pawn in a struggle. Marxism, like so many other white institutions, has chosen to understand the black situation only in so far as it is immediately useful. The Marxist attempting to slot the Negro into a stereotyped dogmatic part of a historical process is, from the Negro's own point of view, irrelevant. Blacks are not going to achieve their identity through Marxism nor – Ellison seems to be saying – is it a force through which blacks and whites may learn to live together.

The second solution – an alternative to the Brotherhood – is presented in the splendidly colourful character of Ras the Destroyer, a West Indian militant leader who pedals an exotic brand of Afro-Americanism; he has his finest and most typical moment during the riot when, dressed as an Abyssinian chief and mounted on a milk horse, he charges the predictably bewildered police with sword and shield. Plainly Ras in his present form does not offer much in the way of practical help, and the hero finds his message of hate and destruction abhorrent. Yet there is something decidedly powerful in his celebration of black pride in his urging blacks to be black. He has an especially strong effect on Clifton, the hero's friend, who seems to have all the qualities of a black leader but who, after a session with the howling Ras, drops from sight until – in the novel's bitterest scene – we find him on a street corner selling Sambo dolls:

> ... which some mysterious mechanism was causing to move up and down in a loose-jointed, shoulder-shaking, infuriatingly sensuous motion, a dance that was completely detached from the black mask-like face. It's no jumping-jack, but *what*, I thought, seeing the doll throwing itself about with the fierce defiance of someone performing a degrading act in public, dancing as though it received a perverse pleasure from its motions.

Unable to accept either the Brotherhood or Ras, Clifton has been thrown back into the black's classic way of tolerating the intolerable – mocking himself, accepting the white-imposed self-image and, by developing the cruellest sense of self-irony imaginable, learning to live with the unliveable. Yet this is a retreat to the position of movement/non-movement, as described before. It also leads to the self-destructiveness that sociologists have so frequently observed in ghetto life; Clifton gets himself shot by a policeman in a way that is tantamount to suicide.

A more sophisticated version of Clifton's behaviour – the third solution, and a clearer alternative to Ras and the Brotherhood – is to be found in the Rhinehart episode. The hero finds that by altering his appearance he can be taken for the Negro 'ace', the ghetto 'stud', Rhinehart, who – sharp and smooth and slick, his finger in a dozen plump pies – can stand outside the whole turmoil and *live* for himself. The snag, though, is that Rhinehart has no self to live for; in the last analysis he is a game player, another Negro acting out an (albeit rarified) fantasy – pimping while ghettoes burn. In order to exist, Rhinehart must do what all Negroes in the novel have been forced to do: he must pretend; he must pretend not to be an individual.

Here Ellison touches on an area that is particularly important to

many black American writers. In order to achieve individuality
the Negro must celebrate his blackness; this must, given the prevailing nature of white consciousness, involve a group effort of
some kind. Yet the group efforts that are available either choke
individuality (as in the case of the Brothers) or provide a bogus
form of black identity (as does Ras the Destroyer). Paradoxically,
however, it seems that the Negro cannot simply step aside and *be
himself* since his blackness continually limits what sort of self he
can be. In the light of this, it is interesting to see how Ellison
handles the question of individuality in the prologue and epilogue
which frame the action.

The prologue sets the tone of the novel and uncovers a number
of interesting points. The Invisible Man is inhabiting a cellar in a
border area' where a white neighbourhood touches Harlem; in
an anticipation of the light/darkness symbolism, which Ellison
repeatedly uses, the hero has turned the traditional blackness of
underground into a blaze of light.

'... there are exactly 1,369 lights. I've wired the entire ceiling,
every inch of it. And not with fluorescent bulbs, but with the older
more-expensive-to-operate kind, the filament type. An act of
sabotage you know.'

The sabotage is at least two-fold – 'at least' because one of the
novel's best features is the expansiveness of its symbolism; the re-
reader continually finds fresh unnoticed patterns. First, the
Invisible Man is stealing the supply from the Monopolated Light
and Power Company – 'I use their service and pay them nothing
at all, and they don't know it' – so there is a literal economic form
of sabotage going on; the exploiting monopoly is itself being
undermined and exploited. But we are also dealing with the
sabotage of society's beliefs about light and darkness, visibility
and invisibility. Monopolated Light and Power dispenses actual
light but moral darkness; it stands for the society which forces the
Negro to behave as if he is invisible – to keep his eyes down, him-

self out of 'white folk's' way and his individuality non-existent to the point of transparency. It is Monopolated Light and Power which keeps the black in darkness. Yet here the Invisible Man uses the institution's own weapon against them. True he has been driven underground (we learn in the last pages of the book that he has fallen through a manhole into the basement on the night of the Ras riot), but he has used the experience. 'I myself, after existing some twenty years, did not become alive until I discovered my invisibility.' In short, he has at last learned how society treats him, has at last learned that to others he is invisible and that *whatever visibility he achieves must start from here*, whatever individuality he discovers must paradoxically come from the knowledge that society wishes to deny it.

Not everyone will agree with my analysis here and some may find the prologue and the epilogue at once pretentious and simple-minded. The symbolic interplay of light and darkness seems liable to endless interpretations, none of which appears to have much connection with the hero's apparently naïve comments about future action.

'... my problem was that I always tried to go in everyone's way but my own. I have also been called one thing and then another while no-one really wished to hear what I called myself. So after years of trying to adopt the opinions of others I finally rebelled ... So I took to the cellar; I hibernated. I got away from it all. But that wasn't enough. I couldn't be still even in hibernation.'

The Invisible Man may be going his own way, but what way is that? After the specific itemisation of society's oppressions of the individual, how can the mere advocacy of individualism offer any sensible alternative? The charge is not entirely without basis, although an answer can be found – one which involves two classically Negro ingredients: the blues and a slave.

Ellison is himself a musician and, from that first moment in the prologue when we encounter him listening to Louis Armstrong, the blues are an important theme. Like so many of the novel's best features, the blues have no precise dogmatic function; here, as in life, music is a system of punctuation, a commentary, a release of energy; as in black life, the blues are the natural expression of black emotion and therefore the most typically indigenous Negro art form. But, if one should not dogmatise about its role in the novel, there is no doubt that it occurs at crucial moments and is of great importance. At Clifton's funeral:

> [an old man] sang with his whole body, phrasing each verse as naturally as he walked ... Even white brothers and sisters were joining in ... Something deep had shaken the event, and the old man and the man with the horm had done it. They had touched upon something deeper than protest, or religion ... It was not the words, for they were the same old slave-borne words; it was as though he had changed the emotion beneath the words.

What Ellison seems to be advocating in that last sentence is a transformation of consciousness – not so much consciousness of anything as much as consciousness *itself*; the blues shows the presence in the old man in the black *and* white crowd of a state of being which transcends 'words', that is, dogma, theory, sociologised explanation. This vaguely mystical proposition receives a more practical twist in the epilogue:

> I've come a long way from those days when, full of illusion, I lived a public life and attempted to function under the assumption that the world was solid and all the relationships therein. Now I know men are different and that all life is divided and that only in division is there true health.

Superficially that seems unpleasantly close to a doctrine of *laissez-faire*, an acceptance of a segregated *status quo*; a counsel of advanced Tomism – live in yourself, do not worry too much about illusion-ridden life, accept the divisions that exist.

Yet what Ellison offers is more positively and possibly practical than that; he is in fact proposing the vitalisation of the blacks' ambiguous position:

The very act of trying to put it [the story] all down has confused me and negated some of the anger and some of the bitterness. So it is that now I denounce and defend, or feel prepared to defend. I condemn and affirm, say no and say yes, say yes and say no. I denounce because though implicated and partially responsible, I have been hurt to the point of abysmal pain, hurt to the point of invisibility. And I defend because in spite of all I find that I love. In order to get some of it down I *have* to love. I sell you no phony forgiveness, I'm a desperate man – but too much of your life will be lost, its meaning lost, unless you approach it as much through love as through hate. So I approach it through division. So I denounce and I defend and I hate and I love.

Here the Negro is learning to live through ambiguity, but in a *different way*. First, he has accepted and recognised the ambiguity for what it is – many-sided. As with so many other problematic things in life, the Negro's position has glory as well as shame; to present the black condition as one only of defeat is to deny his humanity; to present the necessity of black men and women living through hate is as humanly impossible as their living only through love. The fact is that the black person is a person who must at all costs accept his personality; he must be *visible* – visible as *someone* who loves or hates or has ideas about division; visible not as a statistic or sociological phenomenon but as an individual coping like other individuals with the impositions of society, and in this case living through all sides of his ambiguity. Of course, what Ellison implies in *Invisible Man* is that this is exactly how the American Negro has come up from slavery. The blues shows this; as one critic has pointed out, the blues thrives on ambiguity; by a series of ironic shifts and juxtapositions it transcends the painful conditions with which it deals, it neutralises one emotion with another. The blues, therefore, is an example not only of the subtlety of the Negro's artistic understanding but also of his capacity to survive (the quality which white writers like Faulkner so much admire); to illuminate the darkness. Yet there is another side to the blues – less readily admitted but still there. The blues

an also be masochistic; to paraphrase the Invisible Man on a
different subject, the blues can be a way of making love to your
sickness. Again, we see the Negro ambiguity – that which feeds
also eats away; that which celebrates the endurance of suffering
calls up more suffering to be endured. But, says Ellison, so what?
When has life not been ambiguous for everyone? Is not America
an ambiguity and the Negro a part of it? If it comes to that *is not
the white man a part of the Negro ambiguity?* And here we touch on
the experience of the slave – the second classically Negro in-
gredient.

The slave in question is the hero's grandfather, who throws his
family into consternation with his death-bed exhortation:

'. . . I never told you but our life is a war and I have been a traitor
all my born days, a spy in the enemy's country ever since I give up
my gun back in the Reconstruction . . . I want you to overcome
'em with yeses, undermine 'em with grins, agree 'em to death and
destruction, let 'em swoller you till they vomit or bust wide open.'

The family is aghast; whatever else this may be, it is not con-
ciliatory talk. The question of what exactly the old man may have
meant is repeatedly raised in the novel, forming almost a test for
the hero, for we are certainly intended to see the old man as the
repository of some ancient racial truth. Thus, although we can
never be absolutely sure of an interpretation, it is interesting to
find the hero in the epilogue setting off a series of fascinating
possibilities. The Invisible Man moves from the thought that:

'. . . hell, he *must* have meant the principle, that we were to affirm
the principle on which the country was built and not the men, at
least not the men who did the violence . . .'

to the possibility that 'we were the heirs who must use the principle because no other fitted our needs,' – that is, *practically* an
American social future is naturally and sensibly the only one that
will face the American Negro. But, further even than that, he feels
that the Negro bears a special *American* responsibility because,

by another paradoxical quirk, he is more capable than the white
of being American:

> ... older than they, in the sense of what it took to live in the
> world with others and because they had exhausted in us, some –
> not much, but some – of the human greed and smallness ...

Thus:

> ... weren't they their own death and destruction except as the
> principle lived in them and in us? ... Weren't we *part of them* as
> well as apart from them and subject to die when they die? I can't
> figure it out; it escapes me.

So the final Negro ambiguity is that, however much America
has abused him, he is still American; they – whites and blacks –
are going to survive together or go down together. The problem
is not easy; Ellison cannot figure it out and is honest enough to
say so, but since the Negro is there the white American must
relate to him as an individual or the whole nation and its principle
are doomed – and it is a principle worth saving.

Invisible Man is an extremely important novel and a great deal
more could be said about the richness of its texture and the
threads that go to make it up. Whole chapters could be written on
Ellison's use of dreams, of ritual, of jazz. Two points can be made
here about Ellison's talent, both concerned with his imagination.
First, the success of the novel depends very much on the *living*
nature of Ellison's symbolism. Here one is reminded of Dickens;
like Ellison, he can move from one kind of imaginative construction to another without any self-consciousness or strain; again,
like Ellison, he can create a world of intense and immediate
realism (totally representational realism) in a chapter that contains
the wildest flights of fancy, and the two need not clash at all. This
quality is rare and growing rarer; it is ironic that, although modern writers need increasingly to deal with ideas, their very
consciousness of the need inhibits the spontaneity of the ideas'
portrayal. Ellison is spared, and spares us, this. Critics who grope

for a way of describing the odd transference of one type of scene to another (as when in the middle of a sociological discussion the Marxist leader, Jack, grotesquely loses his false eye!), and find even the term 'surrealism' inadequate, are merely paying tribute to the scope of Ellison's imagination.

James Baldwin

A necessarily attentuated treatment of James Baldwin, though regrettable, has some justification. Although he is a talented prose stylist, too much discussion of his books is likely to spoil them for the reader; his novels are both more delicate and conventional than Ellison's; they depend greatly on the ancient narrative gifts of anticipation and surprise – gifts that go in the telling; and many of his ideas about the black condition are held in common with Ellison and have already been considered.

There are two areas, however, to which the reader's attention should be drawn – Baldwin's treatment of guilt and his treatment of homosexuality. His novels all deal with guilt and the individual's struggle to free himself from it. The guilt is sexual or religious – sometimes both. *Go Tell it on the Mountain*, his first novel, gives one of the best fictional accounts of the role of religion in the American Negro's life, and particularly of the way in which it has enabled him to endure at the cost of his natural independence of spirit. *Giovanni's Room*, in which Baldwin assumes the role of a white narrator, deals with the problems of a man who may be heterosexual when he wishes, but *is* homosexual and guilty about it – a subject that is given wider and specifically racial treatment in *Another Country*. Baldwin's handling of the question of black/white/homosexual/heterosexual relations does not seem to me as crude as has sometimes been suggested. First, in writing about homosexuality, he draws attention to an important social fact – since homosexuals are traditionally persecuted, the Negro homosexual has common psychological and social cause with his white partner. Also in homosexuality the Negro has the opportunity to escape from the sexual *machismo* which white legend has thrust upon the black male. The suggestion that Baldwin is adamantly claiming that homosexuality solves the racial tensions which heterosexuality intensifies does not strike me as quite fair. His books are more problematic and indeed more *individual* than that; when he writes, he uses the point of view of a character – a point of view which may well be fallible (it is not easy for either the homosexual or the heterosexual to see the other 'side' completely fairly) and which Baldwin rarely offers as universally true.

At any rate Baldwin must be given credit for bringing into the open the erstwhile suppressed question of homosexuals as a minority group. The 1960s showed a great development here; homosexuals have come out of hiding and have gained their first genuinely public recognition; concealment is no longer absolutely necessary. The literary consequences of this are debatable, for the phenomenon is too recent to pronounce upon. The novels of James Purdy illustrate this; although their (white) author can 'come clean' about the existence of homosexuality, the signs of its suppression and repression are still present. His most famous novel, *Malcolm*, makes use of this, dealing as it does with a fifteen-year-old boy's fear of his homosexual tendencies; but in *Cabot Wright Begins* and in *Eustace Chisholm and the Works* sex is gothicised into violence – in one case expressed in rape, in the other in disembowelling. Purdy is certainly an impressively stylish writer in the main and odiferous stream of black comedy, but his books raise the interesting question of whether in literature suppression is not sometimes a good thing; whether specifically the homosexual does not reproduce in his works the sense of electric suppression imposed on him by society, a quality which, once removed, may remove also the immediacy of his problem and possibly the writer's own homosexuality. In Truman Capote's *Other Voices, Other Rooms* the delicate coolness of the author's prose allows the reader – that is to say, the sexually 'normal' reader – the breathing space needed to take in and appreciate Capote's weird relationship of boy and transvestite.

The mention of Capote and Baldwin raises an interesting point about the problems of writing fiction that deals, on the inside or the outside, with social minorities. Most good writers do not want to be concerned with any one topic or issue; however much a given subject may matter to them, they want a wider recognition of their individual abilities. Thus, the Negro or the homosexual or the Jew wants to write about the immediate fact of his nature that society attacks, but he also wants something beyond that – to be a writer as other writers, different as an individual, of course, but concerned with the whole world of human experience from no less authoritative, no less truthful, a standpoint. Yet one of the features of being the member of a minority group is that, within certain flexible limits, one continually feels the presence of minority responsibility; one *should* go on drawing the attention of rheumy-eyed indifferent society to the problems of being a Negro, a homosexual, a Jew. Obviously there is a potential clash here in artistic intentions – a clash which can only be solved by that rare sort of talent that (like Dickens or Faulkner) is able to go on writing interesting variations on the same theme. Perhaps then it is not surprising to find that Baldwin and Capote take to mutant versions of journalism. In Baldwin's case this is superficially more understandable; the late 1950s and the 1960s saw a great change in the Negro's struggle for social and political identity, and it is natural that a man who cares so much about everyday facts should decide to write about facts every day. Yet one still senses in Baldwin's change the conviction that there is only so much to be said artistically about any one social issue and after a while it is time to treat fact as fact. Capote's case is rather different if only because he moves not into fact exactly but into a sort of grey border area which we, along with other commentators, may as well call para-fiction. *In Cold Blood* not only hovers on the fact/fiction border but establishes a separate country in which the two are indistinguishably mingled. Capote deals with an actual – and particularly bloody mass murder – and his attempt to understand the psychology of the killers is laudable; yet the method he chooses is essentially that of the novelist and the end result is to mulch criminological truth and artistic fiction. The phenomenon here is extensive and, from the point of view of minority fiction, important. The 1960s saw a significant growth in a form of impressionistic literary journalism – of which Norman Mailer and Thomas Wolfe are the most famous exponents. Mailer appears to have abandoned the writing of actual novels to produce, in books like *Armies of the Night* and *Miami and the Siege of Chicago*, techni-colored novelistic impressions of matters of contemporary concern. I for one am convinced that this change in Mailer comes not from a drying up of talent (although his novels are admittedly not *that* impressive), nor purely from the desire to make more money, but from the conviction that the novel is no longer adequate to convey the immediate concerns of the moment; in Mailer's case, these concerns are the possession of a coalition of minority groups – the young, the intellectuals, the Vietnam war protesters. These are groups whose needs cannot be satisfactorily changed through art (art takes too long, it is too reflective, it dallies too much with imaginative truth), yet whose 'facts' must be presented with the tension, the force, the *care* of art, for that is the only way they will get immediate attention. It can, of course, be argued that this 'para-fiction' is part of an extensively robust American tradition of interdependence between literary forms. O. Henry, H. L. Mencken, indeed Hemingway himself, all produce journalism that is very like fiction and fiction that is very like journalism; but none of them produces (as does Mailer) a lengthy justification for the mixing of the two forms on the basis of the inadequacy of either.

THE JEWISH-AMERICAN NOVEL

Perhaps owing to the pressures of worldwide anti-semitism, the

1930s saw the rise of at least four important Jewish novelists in America; three of them – Henry Roth, Edward Dahlberg and Daniel Fuchs – are sufficiently neglected and sufficiently good to merit a few introductory words. Henry Roth has written only one novel, *Call it Sleep*; in its force and in its production of one single authorial experience, it is reminiscent of *Invisible Man*; racially archetypal completeness of the experience may have been the reason for the writer's inability to complete another novel. The protagonist, David Schearl, is the bearer of his immigrant parents' inadequacies; having fled from Europe, they do not understand America, its customs or its language; they have carried their Jewishness from one form of exile to another. Growing up amidst the variegated horrors of the streets, David is additionally haunted by the grimmer side of Judaism which, in its postulation of a sort of Judge Jeffries of a God, blends only too nastily with David's own cruelly paranoic father. The novel ends with a peculiar vision; David sticks a metal ladle into an electrified crack between streetcar rails, receiving a shock which – presumably – purges the past and provides him with a species of reconciling vision. All of this raises some interesting points which recur throughout Jewish-American fiction. First, the parental question where, as if in some reversal of classic tales, we find the strong-but-weak father paired off with the weak-but-strong mother. In other words, the father's avowed masculine strength as provider and head of the family (always heavily stressed in Jewish culture) is diminished and twisted by the historical persecutions of society; the mother, traditionally the submissive partner (in strict Jewish synagogues the women are segregated from the men), the raiser and teacher of children, is forced to teach strength according to a continually weakened model and, in a life of social persecution, to assume the strength which the model does not provide – hence the managing mother so prevalent in Jewish fiction. Yet such is the inherent cohesiveness of Jewish culture that the family remains the unit of survival, although the very qualities by which it survives are dangerously likely to be those that keep it down. Thus, in a country which preaches the possibility of success, the traditional ambition of the Jew is given an added immediacy. Traditional Jewish strengths *may* now be weaknesses; the specifically Jewish parts of Jewish experience are now to be challenged – the protective family which equips the hero for the world may be destructively insular; the capacity to endure suffering may, as with the Negro, invite suffering and bring not endurance but masochism – the Jew, instead of being in flight from society's persecution, may be in flight from his own. Thus, the purging and unifying vision which David Schearl undergoes in *Call it Sleep* is ambiguous; what exactly is it he has escaped from? What is it he wants to expunge – society's treatment of the Jew or the experience of being a Jew itself?

It should be plain from these comments that, given this particular cultural situation, the Jewish novel has ample opportunity for discovering irony. Daniel Fuchs's three novels – *Summer in Williamstown, Homage to Blenholt* and *Low Company* – exploit (usually humorously) the ironies of the Jewish urban situation to be discussed later in the novels of Philip Roth, Saul Bellow and Bernard Malamud. We should first mention two authors – Edward Dahlberg and Nathanael West – who bring Jewish temperamental qualities to novels that for the most part are not about Jews. Dahlberg's *Bottom Dogs* anticipates West's superb *Miss Lonelyhearts* in its application of the Jewish understanding of suffering and deprival, although in West's case the result is on a more powerful and intense level.

Nathanael West
Miss Lonelyhearts is his best-known novel, although critics and readers argue as to whether it is his best. With the exception of his first book, *The Dream Life of Balso Snell* – a pretentiously surrealistic concoction of continental literary influences that ends with one of fiction's most tedious orgasms – he maintains a high and

pretty well equal standard. In *A Cool Million* he produces a Voltairean satire on a specifically American theme (the Horatio Alger strive-and-succeed myth), while in *The Day of the Locust* we find the dank white underbelly of Fitzgerald's *The Last Tycoon* – a pathetic shanty Hollywood of destroyed dreams; a wildly impressionistic slag-heap of lost American aspirations. Each of these books is a stylistic masterpiece; but let us turn to his most famous and most Jewish novel, *Miss Lonelyhearts*.

To speak of this novel as Jewish is contentious; I am not suggesting any limitation of the universality of its artistic achievement but want only to illuminate certain aspects of the work. West was, as his biographer Jay Martin shows, an extremely odd, perhaps even professionally eccentric man; nowhere is this more pronounced than in his attitude to his Jewishness. West was born Nathan Weinstein, the son of well-educated and, until the Depression, prosperous first-generation immigrant Jews. The changes wrought in his name (he moves by stages through Nathaniel von Wallenstein Weinstein to Nathanael West) reflect an extreme development of his family's desire to be upper-class *American* Jews – 'extreme' because West drops out most of the Jewishness, a point that becomes all the more interesting when we consider the religiosity of *Miss Lonelyhearts*.

The hero (who has no private name) is the author of the Miss Lonelyhearts agony column in a newspaper – the job has driven him further into the religious mania to which he has always tended:

> He stopped reading. Christ was the answer, but, if he did not want to get sick, he had to stay away from the Christ business . . . As a boy in his father's church, he had discovered that something stirred in him when he shouted the name of Christ, something secret and enormously powerful. He had played with this thing, but had never allowed it to come alive.
>
> He knew now what this thing was – hysteria, a snake whose scales are tiny mirrors in which the dead world takes on a semblance of life. And how dead the world is . . . a world of door-

knobs. He wondered if hysteria were really too steep a price to pay for bringing it to life.

The message is clear: even if Christianity is a delusively hysterical response to the horror of life might it not be better to embrace it – to embrace anything which might even for a moment alleviate the horror? Miss Lonelyhearts is in the most terrible of positions – that of a man with a religious instinct who believes the instinct to be a sign of insanity; that of a man who feels all the worlds of suffering yet believes that nothing can help it; that of a man who thinks that the only way to react to the awfulness of life is to laugh, yet whose humour turns destructively on itself.

> English humour has always prided itself on being goodnatured and in the best of taste. This fact makes it difficult to compare Nathanael West with other comic writers as he is vicious, mean, ugly, obscene, and insane.

That is West's own advertisement for *Balso Snell*, but it might just as well stand for *Miss Lonelyhearts*, which shares a similar despair at its own self-mockery. What seems at first to be a rather healthy reversal of the cliché that humour should be in general good taste turns out to be itself far from genial. West is not being funny by calling his humour ugly and insane, he is suggesting that life itself is so dreadful that only dreadful humour can be funny about it, and to be funny about anything so dreadful is merely to show the pathetic limitations of humour as a human response. Thus Miss Lonelyhearts, who has originally taken a leaf out of the demonic book of Shrike the Editor (laughing both at the appalling suffering of the letters he receives and at his own neo-Christian desire to help), discovers that 'he could go on finding the same joke funny thirty times a day for months on end'. Here West really reaches sublime heights; for hundreds of years writers have recognised that the same event may be both tragic and wildly funny – West realises that is not necessarily something to be happy about:

[Miss Lonelyhearts' fellow journalists] like Shrike the man they imitated ... were machines for making jokes. A button machine makes buttons, no matter what the power used, foot, steam or electricity. They, no matter what the motivating force, death, love or God, make jokes.

Destructive humour can be just as miserably destructive as the misery it wishes to escape from, and in this West demonstrates one of the governing characteristics of Jewish humour – its acute self-criticism of the very joke that is being made, criticism indeed that in such terrible circumstances a joke should be made at all. The ultimate irony of developing a sense of irony in order to survive is (as shown later by Bellow and Malamud) to realise how little irony helps.

Jewish too is West's treatment of emotion and in particular of sentimentality. Traditionally the Jew has survived the most traumatic sufferings by refusing to duck; the Jew is always ready to feel in situations where others would harden themselves – so much so that too-ready emotionalism has become a stock feature of the anti-semitic joke. There is much of this in Miss Lonelyhearts' attitude to the pain he encounters in those agonising – and brilliantly written – letters. Although he is supposedly the son of a Baptist minister in whom 'no one could fail to recognise the New England puritan', his conscience has little New England rigour about it; indeed, in his desire to feel with the greatest sufferers and to take on himself the responsibility for the pain, he is purest Jew. And here West scores (anticipating Bellow) in realising the limitations of this position. Miss Lonelyhearts lives in terror that his feelings amount only to sentimentality and this is just as well, for there is something suspiciously selective about a world view based on his agony column's gallery of grotesques. It is not that the people who write to him have suffered so much so unfairly (life is full enough of disease and disaster to make that reasonable) but rather that they do not exist outside their pain; like Miss Lonelyhearts they are not characters but suffering kits;

they have to be without any sense of personal responsibility so that they may become the responsibility of Miss Lonelyhearts. Of course, every writer is entitled to his world view and no one should reproach West for choosing a universe of meaninglessly mechanistic suffering. Nevertheless, the reader must see the dangers that lurk here; West is close to the nastiest sort of sentimentality – that which mixes up our guilt with the suffering of others in a way that makes us self-important through other people's pain. It is therefore hugely to West's credit that Miss Lonelyhearts is beset with doubts about his own inclination to suffer, his own desire to take on emotional responsibility for others. This in its turn makes Miss Lonelyhearts more human – there is nothing of the enclosed self-justification that we find in so many modern nay-sayers. Beckett and Kafka – whose vision of a world of meaningless pain West shares – both have a certain quality of narrow-mindedness. Beckett in effect bullies the reader; he absolutely forbids him not to believe Beckett; more than that, he forbids him to qualify even infinitesimally the suffering which he, Beckett, offers. Similarly, Kafka refuses to allow even the *possibility* of the individual successfully resisting the machine; put one ounce of Stephen Dedalus' human cunning into a Kafka character and *The Trial* would adjourn *sine die*. Thus both writers, for all their talent, have a strange element of the masochism which internalises suffering in order to selfishly hold on to it. The reader is therefore compelled into a world of private suffering and then demanded to base a universal case on it. West, though, establishes a broader base; to the very end Miss Lonelyhearts' feelings are ringed with the ironies of their own self-contemplation; his suffering is human because it is ridden with human doubts and hopes and questions. And it does seem to me that this quality of West's comes so exactly from his Jewishness – from living so long with suffering that one understands the self-entrapping complexity of it.

Philip Roth

Of the modern trio of Bellow, Malamud and Roth, the latter is the least impressive, although he has certainly achieved the greatest notoriety – mainly through his 'masturbation novel', *Portnoy's Complaint*, and its dull and silly follow-up, *The Breast*. Although he shares Bellow's interest in the middle-class intellectual Jew, and Malamud's concern with the Jew as representative of certain universal qualities, Philip Roth lacks their depth – lacks, in a way, the depth of their Jewishness. *Portnoy's Complaint* is certainly funny but its humour stays on the surface; he does well to expose the staginess of too archetypally Jewish behaviour (witness the long comic wail that is Portnoy's mother), but he lacks the ability of Bellow and Malamud to see beneath the staginess. It is significant that his best novel, *When She Was Good*, is his most straightforward; it does not try to be clever and is not about Jews; yet this is the only novel in which Roth allows his concern with a traditional Jewish theme – guilt – its fullest, most directly straightforward rein. The book nevertheless lacks something and here Roth is reminiscent of his English contemporaries, Kingsley Amis and John Wain who, like Roth, have a sharp eye for social details and a sharp ear for social or intellectual pretensions; but there is something emotionally stunted about their work; they can deal only with emotions that come through pettiness. Although Roth has much to offer, the same point applies; he lacks the breadth and space of Bellow and Malamud.

Bernard Malamud

Although certainly not inferior to Bellow's, Malamud's art is more straightforward; indeed a case could be made for Malamud as the most powerful *conventional* novelist writing in English at the present time. The only work in which he has tried to play modernistic games – the neo-surrealistic *Pictures of Fidelman* – is not a success and shows how firmly his talents lie in the mainstream of traditional narrative presentation. His two best-known books both deal centrally with a layer of Jewish society which the much more intellectual and cosmopolitan Bellow treats only peripherally – the world of the small, lower-class, truly Jewish urban Jew, still a foreigner struggling to belong in another strange land. *The Assistant* is the story of one such – Morris Bober – a Jewish grocer one step from destitution:

> He was Morris Bober and could be nobody more fortunate. With that name you had no sure sense of property, as if it were in your blood and history not to possess, or if by some miracle to own something, to do so on the verge of loss.

There is no better statement of the temperament of the genuinely downtrodden Jew who feels that any gift exists only to make the subsequent deprival the more bitter. Morris blesses his foul (and Jewish) competitor Karp because 'without him I would have my life too easy. God made Karp so a poor grocery man will not forget his life is hard'.

Morris is the Jew as victim; he has contracted ingrown suffering; pain has become his way of life until he and it are inseparable: the continual series of economic failures that constitute his business, his wife's annoyance at his acceptance of failure, the additional visitation of physical pain – he bears it all in the most horrifyingly resigned way. 'It was terrible but he had feared worse.' To be a Jew then is to suffer; to be a Jew and not to suffer is unthinkable. In the gentile observer, Frankee Alpine, this arouses mixed feelings. On the one hand there is disgust:

> 'His pity leaked out of his pants,' he thought: 'That's what they live for,' Frank thought, 'to suffer. And the one that has got the biggest pain in the gut and can hold on to it the longest without running to the toilet is the best Jew.'

On the other hand there is the feeling that there is something extra-Jewish in the Jews' suffering. Thus Frank exploits Morris with a self-tormenting even-handedness – he robs him but nurses him when beaten up; he steals from the till but makes desperate attempts at reparation. He seduces Morris' daughter, yet tries – at the expense of his own back-breaking everyday toil – to pay her way through college. The novel ends with Frank taking over not only the deceased Morris' store but his entire Jewishness.

> One day in April Frank went to the hospital and had himself circumcised. For a couple of days he dragged himself around with the pain between his legs. The pain enraged and inspired him. After Passover he became a Jew.

On the basis of this splendid and shocking conclusion, critics have held Malamud to be suggesting that all men are Jews; that the Jew is merely suffering man in microcosm. But I think that Malamud goes even beyond this, for he is commenting not only on the spiritual greatness of suffering man but on the peculiar need man has for suffering – as if without it he cannot achieve spiritual greatness. Here Malamud is very much the heir of Dostoievsky who, plumbing the depths, found that man *needed* suffering. Also like Dostoievsky, Malamud worries about suffering's relationship to morality. 'Even when I am bad I am good,' says Frank; in both cases he suffers, in both cases it is pain not ethics that 'enrages and inspires him'; good and bad – however much he might wish otherwise – are confusedly interdependent and in such a situation pain is the only empirical reality. Here Malamud is touching on a question that has become of increasing importance to modern writers – namely, the relationship between morality and emotion, and specifically how, in the face of increasingly weakening socio-moral sanctions, man is to live with the puzzlingly turbulent demands of his own emotions. It is to Malamud's artistic credit that he gives no easy answers, draws no factitious conclusions. The question mark that is left hovering over the whole business merely reinforces the humanity of the story; his characters are real people first and last and, as such, can only understand a small part of the mystery of their lives. To say this is, of course, to illustrate that what matters in Malamud's novel is not any theoretical consideration of the Jew but rather the lives, feelings, thoughts, conduct – the story, in short, of individuals.

It is this same careful itemisation of the individual's make-up that distinguishes his splendid historical novel, *The Fixer* – perhaps, incidentally, the only really successful historical novel written by an American this century. His hero, Yakov Bok, a handyman in Tsarist Russia, is unjustly accused of the ritual murder of a gentile child; like Morris Bober, Yakov suffers a series of minutely portrayed persecutions. In the hands of a lesser writer their depiction would become tedious or literally intolerable; we would turn away from the pressure of his pain or we would choose not to believe in it. But Malamud is (for me anyway) completely successful; *The Fixer* is his *One Day in the Life of Ivan Denisovich*; like Solzhenitsyn, Malamud succeeds by taking infinite pains with infinite patience; his examination of Yakov's persecution, like Solzhenitsyn's account of Ivan's prison day, succeeds through the carefully calm itemisation of the torments both heroes endure. At his best Malamud is one of the most disciplined depicters of suffering so far seen in this century.

Saul Bellow

Bellow is a very different animal. For a start he comes rather late in authorial life to the question of full frontal Jewishness. It is true that one of his early novels, *The Victim* – dealing with the tussle between Asa Leventhal and his paranoic anti-semitic persecutor – establishes one of the recurring themes of minority fiction, that the tormented needs to hate just as much as his tormentor does; but Bellow's other early novels concern victims of a more self-consciously modernistic kind. *Dangling Man*, as its title suggests, treats with modern man in a state of limbo; he waits passively for something to happen to him in the hope that it might make him active. *The Adventures of Augie March* and *Henderson the Rain King* both deal with man's attempts to find his way out of pessimism to some remotely credible optimism – a standpoint that has brought fire down on Bellow from his more militantly negativistic critics. While clearly this theme derives from the minority attitude already discussed, how does one, indeed *can* one, climb out of the set attitudes that keep one suppressed? It is not until *Herzog* and *Mr Sammler's Planet* that the full rich Jewishness of Bellow's concerns are released. (His most recent novel, *Humboldt's Gift*, amounts regrettably to nothing more than a limp re-hashing of these two works.)

Bellow is one of the few modern writers who has the courage to fill his books with characters, ideas, incidents, arguments – without giving the impression (as does Barth) that he is suffering from a form of narcissistic socio-emotional diarrhoea. Both *Herzog* and *Mr Sammler's Planet* are – whatever one thinks of their ultimate value – crammed full of fascinating material for debate: Herzog writing to Adlai Stevenson 'things go on as before with those who think a great deal and effect nothing, and those who think nothing evidently doing it all'; and Mr Sammler seeing everywhere the growth of a new dark Romanticism, a sexual madness overwhelming the Western world – suggest just two of the fascinating questions which pepper both books. Here Bellow has certainly built his reputation on a rock; he is simply one of the few genuine intellectuals writing novels today. By 'intellectual' I do not mean someone who, having decided upon certain ideas, builds his books around them – it would be hard to find a writer who *doesn't* do that; I mean a man who has the capacity to debate, to challenge, to examine whatever mental interpretations of man and his world lie to hand. One of the great defences to be made of Herzog's and Sammler's unsureness about events is that it is earned, it is the product of real independent examination by powerfully independent minds. These are not novels for those who want catchphrase philosophies or knee-jerk thoughts.

Talking of the intellect may give the erroneous impression that these novels are either 'difficult' or 'unemotional'. Sammler, the tired, sophisticated cosmopolitan Jew, defender of civilisation, survivor of Auschwitz, worried by the increasing chaos of the New York in which he will shortly die; and Herzog, the victim of a disastrous marriage, the scholar who has lost his power for scholarship, teetering on the edge of sanity as he writes fascinatingly demented letters to world figures (alive and dead) – both share a surprisingly simple innocence of character and directness of emotional response. Each is caught between the simplicity of his emotions and the complexity of the mind that observes both these emotions and the complex world in which they must strive to find satisfaction. And here Bellow refuses to be labelled; he will neither embrace a naïvely simple philosophy nor abandon himself to a sea of insoluble complexities. At the end of *Mr Sammler's Planet*, Sammler is at the deathbed of the intensely familial Jew, his nephew Gruner; Sammler feels, has always felt, that 'he could not cope with the full sum of facts about him' – Gruner the loyal family man, the decent responsible civilised Jew is also the man who does abortions for the Mafia; Gruner the Mob Doctor. After his death Sammler prays for Gruner, prays to a God whose existence he doubts, out of his own lack of understanding. In many writers this action might be escapist, an abandoning of responsibility to a notional father-figure, but Sammler is different. His prayer – like Sammler himself – is characterised by a scrupulous dignified humility; he talks to God *in case he is there and for Gruner*; the prayer does nothing to solve the nightmares of the modern world nor to gain Sammler relief from them; it is a very unselfish, independent, adult, and sensible prayer. Herzog's behaviour is similar. At one point he finds himself at mass with his appalling wife, who is, at this stage in the novel, his mistress and a temporary convert to Catholicism. 'He was a husband, a father. He was married, he was a Jew. Why was he in Church?' – or, one might add, anywhere, so thoroughly is Herzog lost in the maelstrom of competing thought and emotion. Having strayed into a court of law, Herzog witnesses a case of pitiful child abuse:

I fail to understand! thought Herzog . . . of course he really knew better – understood that human beings *would* not live so as to be understood by the Herzogs?

The hopeful end of *Herzog* thus becomes credible because it is posited on this very failure to understand. Life may be bigger and more complex than Herzog, but Herzog still has to live in it. Nor does this mean an abandonment of life's complexities; while the Herzog 'responsible to civilization in his icy outpost' may belong to his ironically self-tormenting past, the new Herzog, catharsised by his torments, has a new responsibility:

> . . . wondering what future evidence of his sanity, besides re-fusing to go to the hospital, he could show. Perhaps he'd stop writing letters. Yes, that was what was coming, in fact. The knowledge that he was done with these letters.

Herzog is abandoning a false responsibility, for everyone and everything, and assuming a real one – for himself, because only if he is himself uncrushed by life's complexities can he begin to properly cope with them. Herzog has at last freed himself to feel simply about complex things.

Both novels are intensely and intelligently Jewish – on a number of different levels. First, and particularly in the case of *Herzog*, they are steeped in different kinds of Jewish life. The flashback technique, which Bellow, unlike so many authors, uses successfully, helps this; so in successive pages dense atmospheric combinations of Jewish worlds can be seen through a series of archetypal (and usually very funny) characters – Zelda, the Jewish-American princess: 'a girl in Zelda's view had a right to expect from her husband nightly erotic gratification, safety, money, insurance, furs, jewellery, cleaning women . . .'; Sandor Hemmelstein, the lawyer who has built a career on his Jewish-ness: 'I grew up on Sangamon Street, remember, when a Jew was still a Jew' and on the – purportedly – wartime loss of his chest ('He had probably been a sort of large dwarf when he enlisted,' says bitter Herzog) – these figures of urban Jewish affluence are contrasted with the rigours of Herzog's early childhood, the slums of Canada, bedless Jews glad to be sleeping on sacks:

> Mamma's brother Mikhail died of typhus in Moscow. I took the letter from the postman and brought it upstairs . . . It was wash-day. The copper boiler steamed the window. She was rinsing and wringing in a tub. When she read the news she gave a cry and fainted. Her lips turned white. Her arm lay in the water, sleeve and all . . . I was terrified when she lay like that, legs spread, her long hair undone, lids brown, mouth bloodless, death-like. But in the morning she cooked the oatmeal nevertheless. We were up early.

The fact that the same man who produces such dead-centre prose on *this* form of Jewish experience also writes such marvellously funny cosmopolitan stuff – 'Teeth like that deserved a saner head' (Sammler on a demented Zionist) – speaks tellingly for the breadth of Bellow's observation and his understanding not only of the Jewish world but of the greater world in which the Jew must find his place.

The future of minority fiction is problematic. As we have seen, no sooner does a writer embrace a cause than he feels the desire to be an individual distinct from it – or at any rate not wholly dependent on it. This has led, amongst other things, to a certain intermingling of minority attitudes; although it is true that the oppressor traditionally projects his wishes/desires/fantasies on to the oppressed, the process does not take place without some reciprocal influence. Now any American with the remotest pretence to articulacy uses both Negro and Jewish slang; more than that, he uses it to describe Negro or Jewish concepts which he now realises exist in his own white gentile life. Quite how far this development will be cross-fertilising, how far it is merely fashionable, remains to be seen. Equally problematic is what will happen when Jews stop writing Jewish novels and blacks cease producing black fiction; will the result be the loss of existing identities or the emergence of new ones? If it gives us another Ellison or another Bellow, perhaps the question will not matter.

CHAPTER 5

Popular Fiction

The use of the term 'popular fiction' in a chapter heading is contentious. It implies that there is a clear distinction to be made between works which the general public acclaims and works of genuine literary merit – a distinction that hardly applies in the case of Margaret Millar or Patricia Highsmith. It also implies that what the general public likes is by any real artistic standards inferior – yet Hemingway and Fitzgerald both enjoyed literary merit and a wide popularity.

However, although 'popular' has its pitfalls, it is nevertheless used widely enough to merit our attention. For, apart from the intrinsic interest of discovering what people actually like – as opposed to what they are *supposed* to like – a look at such material often prompts questions about the borderlines between the 'popular' and the 'literary'. Sometimes the most pretentiously artistic books spring from a miscalculated yearning for popularity, and sometimes the most unassuming audience-pleasing hackworks grow beyond readers' and authors' expectations into something peculiarly and profoundly satisfying.

One further problem should be raised regarding popular fiction – namely that there is a great deal of it. Future commentators may discover historical or psychological significance in the epic ramblings of Harold Robbins, the supernatural junketings of W. P. Blatty's *Exorcist*, the disaster chronicles of Arthur Haley or the romantic escapades of Margaret Mitchell's *Gone With the Wind*. Here, however, I have concentrated on the two categories which seem most currently worthy of intelligent interest – the thriller (taken to include all manner of 'detective' writing) – and science fiction.

SCIENCE FICTION

The science-fiction boom in America started during World War II with the publication of the magazine *Amazing Stories*. Science fiction is still principally a short-story form produced in specialist magazines for a highly specialised audience; as with horror stories or what American advertisers still naïvely call 'romance', it caters for addicts. And really the success of its best exponents: Robert Speckley, A. E. Van Vogt, Frederick Pohl, Isaac Asimov, Robert Heinlein, Kurt Vonnegut and A. P. Lovecraft depends partly on the extent to which they transcend their readers' expectations, partly on how far they can satisfy their readers' thirst for technological juice while surreptitiously feeding them subtler nourishment. Yet even if these writers do extend the form, the great mass of American science fiction is enslaved by an audience which is prepared to put up with execrably bad writing, complete ignorance of human character and the most laughably superficial moral assumptions. Basic requirements involve absolutely any projection of the future; there is only one immutable rule – it must have gadgets. Like some terrifying allegorical representation of the American dream kitchen (indeed there may be a sociological point there), science-fiction stories are littered with Freudian gadgets. Machines hack and chop and spin and encase and float and suck and bubble, giving the average reader from Poughkeepsie the sense of power over his increasingly technological environment that he increasingly does not have. In this respect it is worth mentioning how very American is the audience's attitude to technology. For while so many works of science fiction deliver would-be Wellsian warnings about the dangers of machines, these possess little of the emotional force given to the description of the machines themselves; the prevailing attitude to gadgets in science fiction, as in American life, is one of fascination. The American who almost lives in his car, and in his lifetime owns so many cars as to be *blasé* about the whole question, may still regard the knobs and twiddles on his new model with a sort of respectful wonder. This attitude is to be found on a vastly increased scale amongst the followers of science fiction who are often prepared (as in the case of Asimov) to sacrifice absolutely everything as long as a new twist is being given to some particular scientific/technological game. In this respect the readers resemble Western fans who will take anything provided they get a decent re-vamping of the central conventions – the gun-fight, the Indians round the wagon. The rise of science fiction may even mean the end of the Western as a literary form – it is doubtful if anything can kill off its cinematic interest. There is no modern substitute for such writers as Zane Grey or Frank Dobie, who treated the conventions of the Western with a sort of dogged honesty. And while there is a passion for it still at the comic-book level, it may be that the rather angry nostalgia of a writer like Larry McMurtry (the present West betrays all the ideals of the old West – but was the old West ever really true?) heralds the end of the Western as anything but a cultural metaphor to be evoked only with painful irony.

Frederick Pohl and C. M. Kornbluth
The Space Merchants is among the most reputable of recent science-fiction works. In its opening chapter, Pohl and Kornbluth succeed admirably in fulfilling one of the principal requirements for the really demanding reader of this genre – they create the impression of living in a totally different world. This is done by the accumulation of vivid details: the narrator does not shave, he uses depilatory soap, extravagantly rinsing his face with fresh water which only comes in a trickle – salt water being in general use. His

office has the ultimate status symbol – 'every piece of furniture is constructed from top to bottom of authentic, expertised, genuine tree-grown wood'. Cars as such no longer exist, but if you want a ride and you are rich enough you can 'pedal a Cadillac'. Only the rich can afford 'new meat'; school lunches are the packaged nightmare of 'soyaburgers and regenerated steak' plus, of course, a 'kiddiebut cigarette ration'. This use of detail accounts for much of the book's success. A character is described as not having sense enough to come in out of the smog; a specially luxurious dinner consists of sausages and apple sauce, and the world's resources have shrunk until there is very little of anything, including space.

> Oddly the most impressive thing . . . was not the rocket itself but the wide swathe around it. For a full mile the land was cleared: no houses, no greenhouse decks, no food tanks, no sun traps. Partly security, partly radiation. The gleaming sand cut by irrigation pipes looked strange. There probably wasn't another sight like it in North America. It troubled my eyes. Not for years had I focussed them more than a few yards.

The narrator/protagonist Mitchell Courtenay is 'star class', that is, a very important person because he has what has become the world's most important job. He is an advertising executive, in an America entirely governed by the need for industrial consumption. Citizens are now known as 'consumers', the government is entirely ruled by industry: 'He spoke of trouble with the Senator from Du Pont Chemicals with his forty-five votes, and of an easy triumph over the Senator from Nash-Kelvinator with his six'; and the law has become correspondingly totalitarian: 'There was a gasp . . . I was violating the most elementary principle of jurisprudence by informing the accused of the nature of his crime.'

At the same time a guerrilla war is being waged by the 'Consies', a group of militant ecologists absolutely opposed to waste and determined to redeem Earth and save Venus which rival advertising agencies are planning to explore and exploit.

The plot measures Courtenay's gradual conversion to Consiedom and is in part based on his discovery of what life is like for those ordinary 'consumers' whose life has regressed to an almost medieval state, containing (irony of obvious American ironies!) plantations and slaves.

Clearly one of the valid uses of science fiction consists in creating projections of the future which throw light on modern society, and one could legitimately claim that *The Space Merchant* is preventive fiction – written so that its prophecies may not come to pass. The seeds of everything that horrify the reader are already planted in modern society and, in such phenomena as nuclear bombs and germ warfare, have already grown quite enough. Kurt Vonnegut has suggested that science fiction is the only realistic form for the times, since it alone contemplates the uncontemplatable horrors which are not only with us but a fundamental guiding part of our society. If this is so – and, in the face of Hiroshima, Vonnegut is hard to refute – why is there not a great deal more fuss made about a book like *The Space Merchants*? Why all this critical reservation about science fiction?

In the light of this question, let us consider what, as writers, Pohl and Kornbluth can and cannot do. The creation of atmosphere through detail has been established. Equally competent (for the authors are real professionals) is the development of and alteration in the central characters' consciousness. Courtenay begins by believing in the ad-men's fictional packaging of the universe and only completely abandons it at the very end of the novel. Thus the authors, in presenting an internal conflict unusual in the simplistic characters of science fiction, stress the *reality* of the problems in hand – that is, if *we* were in that sort of world, we like Courtenay would be reluctant to believe in its underlying horrors; we would sooner cling to fantasy, just (as Vonnegut suggests) as we refuse to face the underlying horrors of our own actual modern existence. Yet, even if this is subtler than the efforts of most exponents, there is still something severely limiting about the characterisation. It is not just that characters are not fully developed (before now writers have built some very impressive houses out of cardboard); nor that the authors wish to concentrate on the world the characters inhabit rather than the characters themselves. It is not even that the characters exist primarily to illustrate ideas – that, too, has been done well enough and, after all, the ideas *are* important. No, the problem consists in the series of curious lapses and queer assumptions about character which is so regrettably symptomatic of so much science fiction. Let us take as an example the relationship between psychology and people in the novel. The whole panoply of advertising is based on an understanding and manipulation of the unconscious motivation. Yet Fowler Schocken, the appositely named founder of one of the world's great agencies, leaves controlling share in his empire to Courtenay over whom hangs a series of psychological question-marks. The sub-plot involving Courtenay's disappearance into the outer world of Consies and consumers is taken by Schocken to be a fantasy for which Courtenay is given treatment. Now the point is made that Schocken is himself living in a dreamworld, where only that which he wishes to be so is true. Still, his *job* is to use psychology to detect weakness, and he allows Courtenay's weaknesses to elude him too easily; he does not even go through the elementary step of considering them – a step he would insist on for the humblest product. More striking perhaps is the revelatory scene in which Courtenay, kidnapped by a rival agency, is tortured with an accompanying lecture on abnormal psychology: 'We *can* hire a killer if we find one who *likes* being punished. And the best part of it all is, the ones who like to get hurt are the ones who just love hurting others.' Here one is expected to believe that an ad-man, a dealer in unconscious motivation, has never heard of sado-masochism!

> The chronicles of fantastic heroism and abysmal wickedness that crowd our newscasts – I knew from research that they didn't have such courage or such depravity in the old days. The fact had

puzzled me . . . [But] when there are *enough* people, you will always find somebody who can and will do any given thing. Taunton *was* an artist. He had grasped this broad and simple truth and used it . . .

As an explanation, that is nonsense; sado-masochism – or, for that matter, heroism – does not arrive as a result of a population increase; it may become more prevalent because of it but that is a very different point. More ridiculous though is the idea that advertising would not, while digging into the darkest sides of man's nature, have played on sado-masochism long since.

Even the non-addicted reader may fail to note such carelessness, just as he may miss the improbable characterisation of the American president as a figure of a certain virtue and moral authority – how, in Schocken's world, could a man like that become president?! The explanation is simple. Even in a superior specimen of the form, the reader skips over all other elements, the human elements, to arrive at those parts of the fiction which are scientific. And, since the ostensible theme of *The Space Merchants* is the future suffocation of the individual, what are we to make of a book that itself manipulates and subordinates individuals to machines? The answer is that we ought to shut up and enjoy the machines, but that is not a comment that reflects well on the form.

Robert Heinlein

Heinlein's *Stranger in a Strange Land* illustrates most of the same points. The story – which is as complicatedly lumpish as the plot is elementary – deals with the arrival on earth of a man from Mars – not literally a Martian, though there are plenty of those but the child born to members of an earlier human expedition to Mars and raised exclusively by Martians. Owing to a series of legal absurdities, the man (he is rather charmingly named Mike Smith) is in earthly terms the heir to Mars – a fact that threatens the world government's plans for further interplanetary colonisation. He is therefore imprisoned until rescued by Jill, his drearily nubile yet, for a while, strangely chaste nurse; she takes him off into the protection of 'Jubal E. Harshaw, LL B, MD, SCD, *bon vivant*, gourmet, sybarite, popular author extraordinary, and neo-pessimist philosopher', whom we first encounter watching his three secretaries splash in the pool. In Harshaw we find one of science fiction's severest problems – a problem which, apart from the brief characterisation of the president, was absent from *The Space Merchants*: that is, the portrayal of male figures who are unreasonably awarded god-like powers and authority. Obviously future psycho-analysers of the twentieth-century novel will have fun with this particular phenomenon; it speaks of a crying need for father-figures that really are figures rather than fathers – a passionate longing to be under the control of someone who, no matter how many perfunctory genuflections may be made towards his 'humanity', still knows all the answers and will take care of everything. This is a continued feature of science fiction, and some commentators suggest that, when associated with the equally present de-humanisation of women – like Harshaw's three secretaries, they are usually dolls not people – the whole adds up to modern man's panicky flight from the human (ie sexual) re-lationships which science has systematically destroyed into a gloriously infantile world of pre-responsibility where Daddy is always big enough to kill the dragon-shadows on the nursery wall (even if the dragons are now shaped like machines).

Heinlein's treatment of the man from Mars certainly reveals a compelling interest in supermen. It is not merely that the Martians have taught Mike all kinds of usefully supernatural skills (his powers of psycho-kinesis allow him to disintegrate anyone or anything in whom or which he detects wrongness; and, when disturbed or puzzled, he can go into a restful and meditatively informative catatonic trance) but that after a certain amount of Harshaw's tutelage he develops into an extraordinary living myth, going like some inverted Elmer Gantry into the sexual side of the religious revival business. Indeed what Heinlein offers us is not unlike what D. H. Lawrence advocated in *The Man who Died* – a

Christ with a sex life. Sex is at the centre of the religion that Mike preaches – sex as physically involuted as one likes, but burned free of the guilt and hostility with which human beings surround it, sex wishing to acknowledge and praise the God within man. 'Thou art God' is the motto and it is with these words on his lips that Mike finally sacrifices his life – in a way that drips with Christian symbolism.

This account of the book's main *events* gives very little idea of those qualities which, during the last five years of the 1960s, made it into a campus cult novel, but perhaps we can give some indication by looking at the Martian verb which Mike continually uses: 'grok'. Literally it means to 'drink'; but, since drinking is especially holy to Martians, it comes to mean 'perfect understanding' – of a kind which, until Mike's arrival, is beyond human beings:

> 'Grok' means 'identically equal' ... The Martians seem to know instinctively what we learned painfully from modern physics, that observer interacts with observed through the process of observation. 'Grok' means to understand so thoroughly that the observer becomes a part of the observed – to merge, blend, intermarry, lose identity in group experience. It means almost everything we mean by religion, philosophy and science ...

It is imaginative touches like 'grok' that really make the book go – the word was, only a short while ago, continually on students' lips – and one can see in the term how Heinlein has persistently tied his science factor in with parapsychology. Mysticism and genuine science (as opposed to mere technology) are linked by Heinlein in a way that is outside the scope of the more efficient but more literal-minded Kornbluth and Pohl. In this connection Heinlein is associating himself with one of the mainstreams of science-fiction writing: the famous trilogy of C. S. Lewis is seriously religious to the point of being a model of Christian orthodoxy – and an opposition to just such an orthodoxy makes up part of H. G. Wells's motivation.

This is not to say that Heinlein's book is wholly successful; as with most exponents of the form, his characters are poorly drawn; his success sticks at the level of ideas. Even here his Christian link-up is rudely forced, and the sexual side of Mike's religion sometimes seems to exist so that the reader may 'grok' away at one or two corners of sexuality which, by virtue of their suspiciously commercial juiciness, would be best left 'ungrokked'.

Kurt Vonnegut
These reservations about *Stranger in a Strange Land* and *The Space Merchants* – both superior examples of the form – only highlight the unusual artistry of Kurt Vonnegut. This addicts of his work sometimes find irritating: he may be an artist, they argue, but is he *really* writing science fiction? Let us consider the question by looking at two of his novels, *The Sirens of Titan* (1959) and the much more recent *Slaughterhouse Five*.

Manipulation is the most obvious of *The Sirens of Titan*'s many themes. Malachi Constant who – like a good Galactic American – wants to be a really significant messenger, delivering meaningful interplanetary messages, is actually being used by Winston Niles Rumfoord, an ex-man of exceptional powers now scattered through space and time; yet Rumfoord himself, like our entire galaxy, is being manipulated by the distant planet Tralfamadore. Following a series of accidents the Earth has become merely a part of the Tralfamadorian communication system; human beings, human history, human monuments are merely convenient or misfiring examples of Tralfamadorian code. For instance, Stonehenge – one of the beautifully laconic touches in which Vonnegut excels – is really a measage saying 'Replacement part being rushed with all possible speed'.

Here Vonnegut is spelling out one of the immutable characteristics of his world view – the powerlessness of human beings and the utter absence of free will. As one of the Tralfamadorians says in *Slaughterhouse Five*:

'If I hadn't spent so much time studying Earthlings, I wouldn't have any idea of what was meant by "free will". I've visited thirty-one inhabited planets in the universe, and I have studied reports on one hundred more. Only on Earth is there any talk of free will.'

Man is trapped, used, predestined – Vonnegut says so again and again – and the worst part is that, deceive himself as hard as he will, he must go on feeling. In Vonnegut's writing there is no way out of this dilemma; no amount of protective irony or fantasising deception will work against the immutable facts of human feeling in a universe which human beings cannot alter. It is vastly to Vonnegut's artistic credit that there is nothing theoretical about this pain; he is unusual amongst science-fiction writers in that feelings precede ideas about feelings.

The Sirens of Titan is the book which comes closest to being out-and-out science fiction; for one thing, it is set in the future, for another it shares with Vonnegut's first novel, *Player Piano* (itself a sort of gentle re-doing of Orwell's *1984*), a much higher proportion of gadgets than we see in his next three works. These – *Mother Night*, *Cat's Cradle* and *God Bless You Mr Rosewater* – all deal with variations on the theme of life's trapped, suffering pointlessness without recourse to science fiction (although each novel is in a sense anti-Utopian, describing the approaching destruction of life by technology); but it is not until *Slaughterhouse Five* that he returns emphatically to science fiction.

Although Vonnegut himself enters the novel *in propria persona*, the protagonist is the allegorically named Billy Pilgrim:

Billy Pilgrim has come unstuck in time.
Billy has gone to sleep a senile widower and awakened on his wedding day. He has walked through a door in 1955 and come out another one in 1941. He has gone back through that door to find himself in 1963. He has seen his birth and death many times, he says, and pays random visits to all the events in between.
He says.

That quotation is important; first, because it describes exactly the structure of the novel – we jump backwards and forwards with Billy; secondly, because the 'He says' throws into question just what parts of the novel, and what parts of Billy's experience, we should believe. What, for example, about his contact with the Tralfamadorians, who apparently capture Billy and stick him in a zoo along with the nubilely beautiful and similarly kidnapped movie star, Montana Wildhack; Billy apparently oscillates between Tralfamadore and Earth (this is possible since Tralfamadore exists outside our notion of time) and takes back to mankind a message of terrible resignation. Here Vonnegut has been very clever; we can either accept that Tralfamadore and Billy's experiences of it are true or that the whole thing is a fantasy released by the multiple horrors of his life – in particular, his survival of the wartime fire bombing of Dresden and of the plane crash that fractures his skull. Vonnegut has taken great pains to sew together the two interpretations – too much so for some addicts, who see the literal reality of science fiction being unnecessarily tampered with.

Vonnegut's writing is always painfully, depressingly humorous and, like Nathanael West's, finds little amusement in the realisation that life is a joke. Also like West, he is always cancelling out one irony with another as if to stress the ultimate comfortless meaninglessness of irony itself. I wonder therefore if *Slaughterhouse Five* may not, in its very open-endedness of explanation, be an anti-science-fiction novel – if Vonnegut is suggesting that science fiction is just as despairing and pointless an interpretation of life as any other. This possibility is backed up by the way in which Vonnegut laughs at so many of science fiction's sacred cows. First, there is the character of the author Kilgore Trout, sci-fier extraordinary:

> 'Jesus – if Kilgore Trout could only *write*!' Rosewater exclaimed. He had a point: Kilgore Trout's unpopularity was deserved. His prose was frightful. Only his ideas were good.

187

That could be taken as a mild joke at other science fictioneers' expense, particularly when one learns that Trout has written about seventy-five books, none of which has made money. But the more one hears of Trout the more he seems like Billy – that is, someone trying to invent another world which will persuade man to go on with the absurd business of living in *this* one:

> '... they were trying to re-invent themselves and their universe. Science fiction was a big help.' – a help because it gives man back his delusions.
>
> The book was *Maniacs in the Fourth Dimension*, by Kilgore Trout. It was about people whose mental diseases couldn't be treated because the causes of the diseases were all in the fourth dimension, and three-dimensional Earthling doctors couldn't see the causes at all, or even imagine them.
>
> One thing Trout said that Rosewater liked very much was that there really *were* vampires and werewolves and goblins and angels and so on, but they were in the fourth dimension. So was William Blake, Rosewater's favourite poet, according to Trout. So were heaven and hell.

Trout apart, Vonnegut gives a number of twists to science fiction's tail. The very little-green-menishness of the Tralfamadorians is almost a deliberate affront to the form's ingenuity. 'Dammit,' Vonnegut might well be saying, 'if you want men from outer space then you can have the tritest ones that anyone ever thought of.' And certainly, by *Slaughterhouse Five*, he is paying no attention to the technological virtuosity so beloved of other authors. Significant, too, is the complete absence of science fiction's beloved father-figures (Vonnegut has produced the last word on this subject at the end of *Cat's Cradle* when he thumbs his nose at what in the novel passes for God). Absent also is the yearning for a semi-pastoral golden age that the fascination with technology so often reveals. Here too, Vonnegut may well be having a grim joke at the form's expense:

Tralfamadorians, of course, say that every creature and plant in the universe is a machine. It amuses them that so many Earthlings are offended by the idea of being machines.

So much for science fiction's great concern of the individual's ultimate supremacy over technology; man is himself (the grimmest joke of all) just so much technological equipment. And perhaps this relates to one final irony: it does not matter which interpretation of Billy's life we take – whether Tralfamadore is real or fictional – because either way man's fate is just the terrible same.

It is debatable whether Vonnegut can be considered a science-fiction writer, a writer who occasionally exploits science fiction or an anti-science-fiction writer. What is not in question is the humorous, pseudo-flip, edgily throw-away but absolutely serious quality of his writing. Even if the reader does not like what Vonnegut does, he will concede that it is done well. This should not be interpreted as a critical blank cheque; he teeters frequently on the brink of sentimentality, and his style has a naïve quaver to it – this he would neither deny nor be ashamed of, but for many readers it makes his books almost perversely sympathetic. Of all the writers who concern themselves with science fiction, Vonnegut's is the voice which most consistently, and in genuinely artistic terms, says important things about the world we live in.

Themes in science fiction

Frank Herbert in *Dune* and *Dune Messiah* has created an epic on a desert planet, heavily interlarded with references to chronicles, rituals and traditions. Mythological material of another kind is used by Philip Jose Farmer, who has written a series of novels starring Blake's pantheon, while his Riverworld trilogy re-incarnates – among others – Mark Twain and Cyrano de Bergerac! Of perhaps more specifically topical interest is Thomas M. Disch's *Camp Concentration* which, in its ingenious handling of mind control and manipulation, resembles *The Space Merchants*.

Telepathy is taken on to a further level by Alfred Bester; in *The Demolished Man* and *Tiger, Tiger*, he investigates the deeper psychic transformations that interplanetary travel would involve.

With regard to the treatment of minority issues, it has been suggested that Samuel R. Delaney, in *Babel 17* and *The Einstein Intersection*, is actually writing an elaborate allegory of the problems of being black in America (he is black himself); while, in *The Left Hand of Darkness*, Ursula Le Guin has created a world peopled – in the best non-sexist way – by beings who can be both male and female and who are appalled at the idea of existing, like humans, in a constant sexual (and chauvinist) rut; the point is well taken, given the sexual attitudes of so much science fiction, as in the case of Heinlein. More specifically reminiscent of Vonnegut in the internal criticisms he makes of science fiction is Norman Spinrad; in *The Iron Dream* he provides a witty and disturbing analysis of some of the fascist nastiness which tends to creep in to altogether too much modern science fiction which for many readers makes his books almost perversely sympathetic. Still, among writers who treat at all with science fiction, his is the voice which most consistently, and in genuinely artistic terms, says important things about the world we live in.

DETECTIVE FICTION

Detective fiction has been an established American form for far longer. As early as Edgar Allan Poe's *The Murders in the Rue Morgue*, one can discern the two principal elements that were to develop along diverging paths in the twentieth century – the tightly composed puzzle and the atmosphere-creating thriller. But Poe was writing stories which happened to be about crime; detective stories, as such, did not flower fully until the 1920s – in the first of the two decades now known as the Golden Age of the detective story.

This was the era of the puzzle-type of detective story; the

reader is treated fairly and given all the clues that the investigator has, deriving the chief source of pleasure from working out the puzzle and an intellectual satisfaction from outwitting the author by guessing the criminal (almost always a murderer) before the last chapter's revelations. In America, the king of the 1920s in this form was undoubtedly S. S. Van Dine, whose revolting hero, Philo Vance, is both a preposterous member of the English aristocracy and a monster of erudition. Van Dine was himself a journalist and an art critic who did his successful best to pump everything he knew into his books. He was a superb plotter, however, and the snobbery and pretentiousness of his books were not out of tune with the period. The mental discipline demanded by his novels is more important than his attitudinising, and we thus encounter one of the critical defences for detective fiction – that, in a world whose writing progressively detaches itself from the intellect, detective fiction compels us to think. (Science fiction, on the other hand, for all the mental overtones of its nomenclature, does nothing of the kind; it requires us only to respond emotionally to the thinking of others.)

Van Dine was one of the first professionals; writing was a business to him. The consequences of this are important; for, while one often admires the technical efficiency of detective writers, their work sometimes has the air of a product, whose real function is to be packaged and sold. How many detective *novels* can you remember without prompting? It is much easier to recall authors than books, which shows the great importance of the formula; it seems a pity that so much thinking can be so unmemorable.

This is particularly true of Ellery Queen, whose first books were published in the late 1920s; his career continues up to the present, even though one of him (he is two people) is now dead. His detective novels are endlessly inventive; his puzzles involve baffling reversal upon baffling reversal, and at times verge on being clever-clever. (In one case the criminal has laid down clues which only Ellery Queen would be clever and erudite enough to follow!) Heavily influenced by Arthur Conan Doyle, Queen has created a superhuman detective, aided by a Watson figure (his father). At a crucial point in the story the detective turns patronisingly to the audience and tells them they now have all the information they need to solve the mystery. The trick is as maddening as it is fascinating.

Although the Queen books have, over the years, emphasised the detective less and the atmosphere more, they remain primarily excellent examples of the formula puzzle story. In this category, too, is Rex Stout, whose fictional career began in the 1930s. His detective is a grossly fat, orchid-fancying gourmet called Nero Wolfe, who solves his mysteries by flashes of intuition (he certainly cannot have worked them out; plotting is not Rex Stout's strong suit, and clues are as sparse as rain in the Sahara). Stout's characterisation, though superficial, is entertaining, and his books, while not in any sense art, never disappoint.

Erle Stanley Gardner is the formula writer *par excellence*. Investigator Perry Mason and his secretary, Della Street, have been soldiering on unchanged since 1932. Gardner is said to have written 120 books, but the final score may well be higher; they depend for their success on a neanderthal simplicity of pattern.

The puzzle story has of late modulated into one concerning police procedure; focussing on a group of policemen going about their work, it incorporates several mysteries or crimes in one volume. Ed McBain comes readily to mind here, with his splendid observation of investigative detail combined with fascinating vignettes of New York life. A problem of the form, however, is that each book lacks a central focus of attention.

Hillary Waugh also describes a group of police at their work, but confines himself to one case per book. Unfortunately for him, though, his first, *Last Seen Wearing* ... was so good that each subsequent one has been judged against it and found wanting. *Last Seen Wearing* ... is about the disappearance of a girl college student; the suspense of the search for her is excellently created, and the final sentence is a classic.

The other element in detective fiction, the atmosphere-creating thriller, provides fewer restrictions. Works in this form range from the early romances of Mary Roberts Rinehart, in which witless young women get themselves into perilous situations, through the sadistic brutalities of tough private 'tecs to the subtle and disturbing evocations of disturbed mental states, as in the work of Patricia Highsmith.

The highest achievement in this thriller form is undoubtedly Dashiell Hammett's. Hammett refused to accept formula for formula's sake; his eight long years as a detective for the Pinkerton agency gave him insight into criminals and the underworld, including the soft white underbelly of respectable people, and his few remaining illusions would not have covered a postage stamp. In Hammett's fictional world nothing is taken for granted; there are no omnipotent father-figures; erudition is a waste of time; the police are crooked as often as not, and there is no honour among thieves. This in itself would not make his books the masterpieces they are, if it were not for his style – which is often imitated but never equalled. It has something of the muted, astringent quality of Hemingway's prose, without the sometimes indulgent emotional undertones. His greatest achievement is probably *The Glass Key*; *Red Harvest* and *The Maltese Falcon* are also excellent.

Raymond Chandler, a great admirer of Hammett's, writes in a similar style, though not as well. His work is weakened by his detective, Philip Marlowe, who has something of the superhuman about him; he is involved with corruption but never sullied by it, and he is allowed to remain too detached – almost heartlessly so – from the crimes he investigates. However, *The Big Sleep* is infinitely better than anything, say, Erle Stanley Gardner ever wrote; it is good of its genre, and to say that it does not reach Hammett's heights is not to insult it. Chandler's style is laconic, tending to epigrams in the Hammett mode.

Reminiscent of Chandler is Ross Macdonald, a novelist of the 1950s and 1960s. His detective, the private eye Lew Archer, unfortunately resembles Philip Marlowe in virtue and priggishness, but Macdonald evokes the atmosphere of California – the setting for most of his novels – very well, although his self-conciously sparkling style can be irritating: 'It was a face that had known suffering, and seemed to be renewing the acquaintance.' He is also obsessed by the physical appearance of women. In *The Zebra-Striped Hearse* the murderess Harriet Blackwell is motivated chiefly by hatred of the world because she has a prominent forehead and nose; this leads her to kill three people! However, the main body of Ross Macdonald's work is sound, and he has some understanding of character; this in itself sets him far above most detective-story writers. Perhaps his best book, for anyone interested in following him up, is *The Far Side of the Dollar*.

Ross Macdonald's wife, Margaret Millar, writes haunting psychological thrillers – no 'private eyes' for her. Usually centred on a girl in a situation – such as half-remembering a bad dream – her story begins by being intangibly uneasy and goes on to become downright terrifying. *A Stranger in my Grave* is an excellent example of her best work, but for sheer terror – and psychological insight – her recent *Beyond This Point are Monsters* must be first choice. The book concerns a mother's obsessional insistence that her twenty-four-year-old son, missing for a year in suspicious circumstances, is not, in fact, dead. As it becomes clearer and clearer that he *is* dead, she grows more and more determined not to believe it until, finally confronted by his murderer, a young man his own age who works for her, she decides not to hand him over to the police, but to keep him instead of the son she has lost. The *frisson* of terror this evokes is comparable to that at the end of Evelyn Waugh's *A Handful of Dust*, where Tony Last is left in the jungle, condemned to read Dickens' novels aloud to his captor for the rest of his life.

The queen of haunting psychological thrillers is acknowledged to be Patricia Highsmith. Sometimes no murder takes place; sometimes the hero is the murderer. What she is always concerned with is human personality under criminal stress. *Strangers on a Train*, one of her early books, is among her best-known; also to be recommended are *Those Who Walk Away* and *The Two Faces of January*. In Margaret Millar and Patricia Highsmith we see detective fiction becoming far more like ordinary fiction, and far less formulaic – the concern for the individual reality of situations rather than the distortion of reality to fit wish-fulfilment world views. Dashiell Hammett began the process; and surely the future of detective fiction lies in the direction of realism, whether in the bread-and-butter reporting of police procedural novels or the deeper psychological explorations of the violence so often under the surface of everyday life.

Conclusion

In responding to the toast, 'The Twentieth Century', Senator
Albert J. Beveridge said in part: 'The twentieth century will be
American. American thought will dominate it. American progress
will give it color and direction. American deeds will make it
illustrious.'

In that quotation from the opening section of Dos Passos' *The
42nd Parallel* there is no mention of American literature; it is also
interesting that the long catalogue of heroes and villains in *USA*
contains no writers of significance. America has been slow to
honour her writers and, though she has sometimes rewarded
them with great material wealth, she has not readily granted them
authority, whether artistic or moral. Perhaps this partly explains
the flight abroad – especially to France where a novelist may be
almost as socially secure as a civil servant. Better exile than to be
recognised fully only after your death, like Melville and Whitman.
Perhaps this also explains the American novelist's tendency to set
himself up in another kind of trade – pop-prophet like Norman
Mailer, critic like Robert Penn Warren, journalist like Hemingway, or academic like so many post-war authors. They do not do
this simply for the money; they do it because through their new
occupation they can receive the attention and respect which they
can re-direct towards their own writing. Again and again Norman
Mailer, while preaching about Vietnam or party congresses or
moon flights or Marilyn Monroe, returns to the subject of himself

as a writer, thereby winning for his novels a great deal more attention than they deserve. This attitude may merely be a defence against the anti-intellectual and anti-aesthetic attitudes often found in American society; and perhaps the tendency of novelists to take shelter in universities is a way of getting back at society outside while commanding a sufficiently respectful and attentive audience within.

The usual critical response to this state of affairs is to blame society for being philistine, and certainly the charge has substance. Yet one can sometimes detect in American novelists, for all the century's move away from provincialism, a sense of puzzled guilt as if, whether it be society's fault or their own, they know that their own writing is, by comparison with that of other countries and other times, inferior.

Writers often fear and critics frequently state: that contemporary novelists cannot write like Faulkner and Hemingway; that Faulkner and Hemingway could not write like Melville and Hawthorne; and that Melville and Hawthorne do not really compare with the great classics of other literatures – in short, that the American novel is perpetually deficient.

This attitude, though not expressed so cogently, has coloured a good deal of European critical thinking. It involves the dismissal of most nineteenth-century American novels as crude; the expropriation of Henry James as a European, and the patronising of the occasional work of raw, unformed natural genius, like *Moby Dick*. This attitude has been extended, *mutatis mutandis*, to the American novel of this century; the Americans have now learned to conceal their clumsiness with a good deal of technical gloss, but the 'fact' is that they have no great experimenters like Joyce and Proust, no modern mystics like Virginia Woolf, no notable political analysts like Sartre and Camus, no aggravating geniuses like Lawrence, no calm universalists like Hesse; no imaginative creators of fairy stories like Tolkien. What America does have is a great number of writers of considerable competence – an inexplicably deadly word to critics – decent, hard-working, if rather immature fellows of the second and third rank. When such an argument begins to take notice of Nabokov, it dismisses him as a freak rather than a natural phenomenon – and a European freak at that. When the same argument bothers with Faulkner, it sees him as a modern reincarnation of the nineteenth-century geniuses – exciting, dramatic, even original, but lumpish beyond belief.

Just as this century has provided a necessary revision of Europe's generalising patronage of the nineteenth-century American novel, it is likely that time will do the same thing for the works of the twentieth century – and if this book fulfils no other purpose it is to be hoped that it will have shown the rich quantity of modern American material. It must be admitted, however, that time is a considerable problem; it is not easy to judge works that one is close to. Complicating this is the difference in European and American attitudes; fundamental to the revaluation of the nineteenth-century American novel was the realisation that American realities required a treatment, both in content and style, different to those of Europe. Even if one concedes this point as valid (to some it seems too easy a way out) the difficulty now is deciding what differences in treatment the American novel has required this century, and how far a recognition of these difficulties will raise its standing.

I introduce these questions not to propose solutions, which would involve the writing of another book, but to indicate to the reader how very conditional and personal any of the following points and opinions must be.

Whatever critical standards one adopts, three simple but vital points may be cited in favour of the twentieth-century American novel as a whole. First, it says important things; second, it has produced some important styles; third, it has caught with the immediate texture of life the behaviour, manners and customs of different periods.

Self-evidently, America is of huge importance in the twentieth century not only for itself but for the rest of the world; it is therefore of the most vital importance that the American novel provides a continual revaluation of America. It should be clear from an examination of the authors we have discussed that they are engaged in an actual revaluation, not merely the instant adoption of stock criticisms or fashionable complaints.

Style is a more contentious question. The more definite the style – the bleakness of Hemingway, the ellipticism of Faulkner, the inlaid mosaic of Nabokov – the more it is open to peremptory dismissal, particularly since in so much modern criticism style is treated as if it were at all times inseparable from content and that once an author has been declared 'unsatisfactory' or 'immature' nothing need be said about his language. American writers are given little of the lengthy verbal exegesis given to Joyce, Proust or even to Beckett. Yet this only points up what paradoxically might be described as the spectacular efficiency of twentieth-century American prose style. One is continually impressed by the sheer efficiency of novelistic language in the period, how quietly and unobtrusively it says what needs to be said, and how reprehensibly easy it is to overlook such qualities. Much of the credit for this efficiency should go to the influence of Scott Fitzgerald, for although it is customary to notice his purpler passages he is given little credit for the persistent power of his ordinary narrative; it is significant that in *The Last Tycoon* for all the familiar magic of theme he was producing the most quietly powerful prose of his life.

The third point in favour of the American novel concerns the immediate texture of life.

One of my most vivid memories is of coming back West from prep school and later from college at Christmastime. Those who went farther than Chicago would gather in the old dim Union Station at six o'clock of a December evening, with a few Chicago friends, already caught up in their own holiday gaieties to bid them a hasty goodbye. I remember the fur coats of the girls returning from Miss This-or-That's and the chatter of frozen breath and the hands waving overhead as we caught sight of old acquaintances, and the matchings of invitations: 'Are you going to the Ordways? the Herseys? The Schultzes?' and the long green tickets clasped tight in our gloved hands. And last the murky yellow cars of the Chicago, Milwaukee and St Paul railroad looking cheerful as Christmas itself on the tracks beside the gate.

That is one of the most famous passages from *The Great Gatsby* but no amount of fame, and no amount of repetition, can make it less good. What it illustrates is Fitzgerald's superlative grasp of atmosphere – the ability to make the familiar true and the unfamiliar infinitely desirable. But, more than that, it shows what is universally recognised to be one of Fitzgerald's most characteristic features – the capturing of the exact feel of an exact place at an exact moment. What is less universally recognised is how important this is and how many American novelists do it – though not all as successfully as Fitzgerald. All great writers are rooted in the moment-to-moment process of living and, if the twentieth-century American novel does not always achieve the highest incidence of greatness per page of prose, it certainly has a real grasp of the immediate. No sensitive reader will easily discount the vividness of Fitzgerald's young men on the way to cocktails at the Yale Club, or Steinbeck's Okies choking in dust, or Malamud's fly-blown delicatessen or Ralph Ellison's light-soaked cellar. The American novel this century is alive with the surface of life.

All this is general, and we should remember how specifically America has been attacked, from within and without, this century, and how directly so many of the criticisms affect the reputation of its literature. There is in American life a peculiar combination of the flexible and the intractable, of the ideal and pragmatic, of the hopeful and the despairing, that often baffles foreigner and native alike. Part of this is doubtless due to the relationship in American life between theory and practice. Probably this was in existence before the framing of the Constitution, but it is striking how exactly codified is America's ideal of itself, and how widely varying the application of the code. (There is something in the American character which refuses to recognise that what the Constitution laid down was not what America *was* but what it should become; and no amount of amendments have been able to eradicate that basic confusion in tenses.) This is not so much an accusation of inconsistency as a description of the heterogeneity which makes sweeping statements about the portrayal of American life in literature so questionable.

In the light of this it is interesting to consider briefly two contemporary theorists on the relationship between American life and literature who relate most pertinently to the present and future states of the novel – Leslie Fiedler and Marshall McLuhan.

Leslie Fiedler is without doubt the most decisive living critic of the American novel. His most influential book, *Love and Death in the American Novel*, applied the techniques of psycho-analysis to the whole course of the American novel, and his subsequent books have continued the process, overturning many a household god along the way. He holds that, because of the particular nature of America's foundation and evolution (the psychological make-up of the original inhabitants, the complications of dealing with the natives, man's fear of the size and inherent cruelty of nature, the lingering guilt of the revolutionary no matter how just the revolution), America has produced a literature which mirrors its society's confusion and guilt. This same confusion and guilt is frequently repressed by the conscious minds of writers, only to emerge unconsciously. In consequence, the American novelist can only rarely deal responsibly with sex, marriage, women or race. The best American novelists – talent apart – are therefore those who come to terms most honestly with their own guilt – who admit it and admit the dark side of their own unconscious motivations.

O

Fiedler is certainly brilliant and there can be no doubt that he has grasped an important point about American literature. His insights on many authors are magnificent; for example, his analysis of Faulkner's horror of women – and guilt at his own horror – does much to explain the peculiar intensity of Faulkner's world view. Such examples of the unfairness of men's fictional portrayal of women have paved the way for much of the Women's Liberation Movement's reconsideration of male-female roles in literature.

However, Fiedler is unconvincing when he wishes to make his theories the whole of the law, particularly when this involves the wholesale rejection of certain novelists and certain kinds of novel. He has no patience with optimism; in his *No in Thunder* and *Waiting for the End* he has suggested that the successful novelist must be a nay-sayer – anything else is escapist. Consequently for Fiedler, a great deal of American literature flies out of the window.

The weakness in his argument is that it is based upon dubious premises about both psycho-analysis and life. While he is correct in identifying the presence of man's dark unconscious urges, he fails to acknowledge that these constitute only a certain part of man's unconscious make-up; the whole concept of much psycho-analytic treatment is based on the belief that man is essentially a healthy organism that wishes to heal the various assaults, such as guilt, which are made upon it. The assumption that man's negative and self-destructive urges mean that he *is* negative and self-destructive is no more valid than the assumption that because there is meaninglessness in life, life must in a permanent and absolute sense be meaningless. While one appreciates Fiedler's attacks on the bogus optimism which has often characterised American life and literature, it is unreasonable to claim that all optimism is bogus. And while it is true – as we have seen throughout this book – that the modern writer fears meaninglessness and needs increasingly to come to terms with it, this may prove that he is afraid but it does not prove that his fear is justified.

The ultimate limitation of Fiedler's views is that they restrict the American writer to one kind of belief and one mode of literary behaviour; in short, they take away the very individuality that, for all its lapses in practice, America has always valued. It is noticeable, incidentally, that Fiedler, who is so scathing about escapist optimism, pays scant attention to its nay-saying equivalent, escapist pessimism.

Fiedler also fears for the future of the novel form, and here his views combine the practical and the metaphysical. On the one hand, he cites the fact, which has been worrying novelists and publishers the world over, that fewer and fewer people are reading serious novels; on the other hand, he sees the novel as having already outlived its psychological usefulness.

> What is there for Burroughs to do with the novel . . . nothing, of course but to destroy it; or rather, to make clear that it has already destroyed itself; for it is a form which realised itself in the mid-eighteenth century, precisely at the moment when men became conscious of their unconscious minds and resolved to redeem them. And it is hard to see how it can outlive the faith of the first novelists in the power of reason to know even the irrational. There are various ways to declare the death of the novel; to mock it while seeming to emulate it, like Nabokov, or John Barth; to deify it into a collection of objects like Robbe-Grillet; or to explode it, like William Burroughs, to leave only twisted fragments of experience and the miasma of death.

Without specifically challenging the several value judgements in that quotation (for example, the relationship between reason and the irrational; and the assumption that Nabokov's mockery necessarily means a mockery *of* the form rather than a mockery *in* it), we can again see the narrowness of Fiedler's albeit interesting views. While later in his book he admits that fiction will go on after the novel stops, he never thinks that the novel itself may mutate from within; I feel that this oversight is due to a limited notion of what a novel can or cannot be. So, while no one who cares for the future can or should regard falls in circulation or in sales with equanimity, it is a little too early to go into mourning. The novel has always been an extremely elastic form, so much so that critics cannot even agree on a general definition of it. It may well prove elastic enough to snap back in the face of nay-sayers.

The matter of decline in readership is of particular relevance to the teaching – one might almost say, the apostolic mission – of Marshall McLuhan, for he has invoked the existence of a cultural revolution in which the whole existence of and need for the printed word has been called into question. McLuhan is a great deal more quoted than he is read, and is more of a talisman than a teacher. As Jonathan Miller has shown in his quite excellent study, McLuhan's books are vast haggises of misinformation, spurious arguments, impenetrable jargon and pseudo-science; they also contain phrases of singular brilliance – 'global village', 'the medium is the message' – which have undoubtedly caught the world's imagination. Thus, irrespective of whatever doubts one may have about his work as a whole – many worshippers have no doubts whatsoever, and indeed find doubts immoral – he has, in Miller's words, 'successfully convened a debate on a subject which has been neglected too long'. The subject is the field of communications – the manner, that is, in which we communicate with one another.

Four useful points emerge from McLuhan's variegated works; all of them provide a challenge to the novel form and to our whole notion of apprehending the words on which all literature depends. First, McLuhan everywhere brings out the importance of television and advertising, which he sees not as the traditional bogeyman of modern culture but as a new liberation from the conventional tyranny of the printed word. Secondly, this liberation consists in the employment of all our senses as opposed to the limited quantity employed by the printed word. Thirdly, this has interesting implications for the way in which we read; no one has yet considered that books might be read as music is played, that certain parts might be read faster than others, that some sections should be read *allegro con brio* and others *largo*; in short, that the readership's attitude to the whole act of reading may now be subject to more variations than ever before. Fourthly, McLuhan raises the question of cultural revolution: may we not be passing through a period of revolutionary change in which conventional art forms are going into the melting pot and the entire nature of perception may be altering? McLuhan is not alone in this last point; Charles Reich's *The Greening of America* produces a categorisation of recent perception changes, all of them indicating a new American Romantic revival pointing – the reverse of McLuhan, this – to a cleaner, greener, less technological future.

The moot point here is whether McLuhan and Reich have confused a fundamental change with an alteration in fashion; for, while the 1960s – the period in and about which they write – showed not only an improvement in general American taste but a vastly increasing interest in taste itself, who is to say that the change will not stay at that level – an alteration in style, not substance? McLuhan has shown that serious consideration must be given to the role of the printed word in American culture; it may soon be in the unusual position of having to justify its very existence.

The future of the American novel has, then, a large question mark over it, as large as the question mark that hangs over this century's novelists. Nevertheless, I believe that all art, the novel included, is largely a matter of individual talent; that whatever society does to or says about or imposes on the individual, if he has the gift, there will be his theme. I cannot see that changing; and the only circumstances in which I can envisage the novel's death is if those with talent cease to find its form of any use. I hope that this book will have shown that this particular danger is some way off.

Select Bibliography

Baker, Carlos. *Ernest Hemingway: The Writer as Artist*. Princeton, 1952
Bellamy, Edward. *Looking Backward*. Boston, 1929
Booth, Wayne C. *The Rhetoric of Fiction*. Chicago, 1961
Commager, Henry Steele. *The American Mind*. 1951
Empson, William. *Seven Types of Ambiguity*. Rev ed, 1953
Fiedler, Leslie. *Love and Death in the American Novel*. 1960; *No in Thunder*. 1960; *Waiting for the End*. 1964
Furnas, J. C. *The Americans. A Social History of the United States 1587–1914*. 1969
Geismar, Maxwell. *The Last of the Provincials*. 1959
George, Henry. *Progress and Poverty*. 1879
Lewis, Robert W. Jr. *Hemingway on Love*. Austin, 1965
Miller, Jonathan. *Marshall McLuhan*. 1971
Mizener, Arthur. *The Far Side of Paradise*. Rev ed, 1964
Reich, Charles. *The Greening of America*. 1970
Sanderson, Stuart. *Hemingway*. 1961
Seymour Smith, Martin. *Guide to Modern World Literature*. 1973
Tanner, Tony. *City of Words*. 1971
Turnbull, Andrew. *Scott Fitzgerald*. 1963
Wilson, Edmund. *The Wound and the Bow*. 1941
Wolfe, Tom. *The Electric Kool-Aid Acid Test*. 1968
Young, Philip. *Ernest Hemingway: A Reconsideration*. Rev ed, 1966

INTRODUCTION

Anderson, Sherwood (1876–1941). *Winesburg, Ohio*. 1919
Cather, Willa (1873–1947). *My Antonia*. 1918
Lewis, Sinclair (1885–1951). *Main Street*. 1920; *Babbitt*. 1922; *Dodsworth*. 1929
Hemingway, Ernest (1898–1961). *The Sun Also Rises* (entitled *Fiesta* in Britain). 1926

CHAPTER I: THE TRADITIONAL NOVEL

Fitzgerald, F. Scott (1896–1940). *This Side of Paradise*. 1920; *The*

Beautiful and Damned. 1922; *The Great Gatsby.* 1925; *Tender is the Night.* 1934; Rev ed, 1951; *The Last Tycoon.* 1941

Hemingway, Ernest (1898–1961). *In Our Time.* 1925; *The Torrents of Spring.* 1926; *The Sun Also Rises (Fiesta).* 1926; *A Farewell to Arms.* 1929; *Winner Takes Nothing.* 1933; *For Whom the Bell Tolls.* 1940; *Across the River and Into the Trees.* 1950; *The Old Man and the Sea.* 1952; *A Moveable Feast.* 1964; *Islands in the Stream.* 1970

Waugh, Evelyn (1903–66). *A Handful of Dust.* 1934

Wolfe, Thomas (1900–38). *Look Homeward Angel.* 1929; *Of Time and the River.* 1935

Lewis, Sinclair (1885–1951). *Babbitt.* 1920; *Main Street.* 1922

Stendhal (1783–1842). *Le Rouge et le Noir.* 1830

Flaubert, Gustave (1821–80). *L'Éducation Sentimentale.* 1869

Twain, Mark (1833–1910). *The Adventures of Huckleberry Finn.* 1884

Dos Passos, John (1896–1971). *Three Soldiers.* 1921; *Rosinante to the Road Again.* 1922; *Manhattan Transfer.* 1925; *USA.* 1938

Vonnegut, Kurt (1922–   ). *God Bless You, Mr Rosewater.* (1965)

Mailer, Norman (1923–   ). *Armies of the Night.* 1968; *Miami and the Siege of Chicago.* 1968

Forster, E. M. (1879–1970). *A Room with a View.* 1908

Steinbeck, John (1902–68). *Cup of Gold.* 1929; *Tortilla Flat.* 1935; *In Dubious Battle.* 1936; *Of Mice and Men.* 1937; *The Grapes of Wrath.* 1939; *Cannery Row.* 1944; *East of Eden.* 1952; *Sweet Thursday.* 1954; *Winter of Our Discontent.* 1961

Caldwell, Erskine (1903–   ). *God's Little Acre.* 1933

Kerouac, Jack (1922–69). *On the Road.* 1957

Sinclair, Upton (1878–1969). *The Jungle.* 1906

Faulkner, William (1897–1962). *The Sound and the Fury.* 1929

CHAPTER 2: THE FATE OF THE TRADITIONAL NOVEL

Faulkner, William (1897–1962). *Sartoris.* 1929; *The Sound and the Fury.* 1929; *As I Lay Dying.* 1930; *Sanctuary.* 1931; *Light in August.* 1932; *Absalom, Absalom!* 1936; *The Unvanquished.* 1938; *Go Down, Moses.* 1942

Woolf, Virginia (1882–1941). *The Waves.* 1931

Updike, John (1932–   ). *The Poorhouse Fair.* 1959; *Rabbit Run.* 1960; *The Centaur.* 1963; *Couples.* 1968; *Bech: a Book.* 1970; *Rabbit Redux.* 1971; *A Month of Sundays.* 1975; *Marry Me.* 1977

Lawrence. D. H. (1885–1930). *Lady Chatterley's Lover.* unexpurgated, 1961

Greene, Graham (1904–). *The Heart of the Matter.* 1948

Twain, Mark (1833–1910). *The Adventures of Huckleberry Finn.* 1884

Capote, Truman (1924–). *The Glass Harp.* 1951

CHAPTER 3: FANTASY

Miller, Henry (1891–). *Tropic of Cancer.* 1934; *Black Spring.* 1936; *Tropic of Capricorn.* 1938; *Sexus.* 1949; *Plexus.* 1953; *Nexus.* 1960

Lawrence, D. H. (1885–1930). *Women in Love.* 1920

Joyce, James (1882–1941). *Finnegan's Wake.* 1939

Burroughs, William (1914–). *Junkie.* under pseudonym William Lee, Paris, 1953; *The Naked Lunch.* Paris, 1959; *The Exterminator.* Paris, 1960; *The Soft Machine.* 1961; *The Ticket that Exploded.* 1967

Dos Passos, John (1835–1910) *USA.* 1938

Kerouac, Jack (1922–69). *On the Road.* 1957; *The Dharma Bums.* 1960; *Sartori in Paris.* 1966; *Maggie Cassidy.* 1959

Fariña, Richard (died 1966). *Been Down So Long It Looks Like Up to Me.* 1966

Katz, Elia (1949–). *Armed Love.* 1971

Capote, Truman (1924–). *The Grass Harp.* 1951; *In Cold Blood.* 1966

Pynchon, Thomas (1937–). *V.* 1963

Hawkes, John (1925–). *The Cannibal.* 1949; *The Beetle Leg.* 1951; *The Lime Twig.* 1961; *Second Skin.* 1964

Barthelme, Donald (1931–). *Snow White.* 1967

Brautigan, Richard (1933–). *In Watermelon Sugar.* 1964; *A Confederate General from Big Sur.* 1965; *Trout Fishing in America.* 1967

Barth, John (1930–). *The Sot Weed Factor.* 1960; *Giles Goat-Boy.* 1967

Heller, Joseph (1923–). *Catch-22.* 1961

Kesey, Ken (1935–). *One Flew Over the Cuckoo's Nest.* 1962

Vonnegut, Kurt (1922–). *Slaughterhouse-Five.* 1965

Mailer, Norman (1923–). *Barbary Shore.* 1951

Nabokov, Vladimir (1899–1976). *Lolita.* 1955; *Pale Fire.* 1962; *Ada.* 1969

CHAPTER 4: THE MINORITIES

Didion, Joan (1934–). *Play It as It Lays.* 1971

Buchanan, Cynthia. *Maiden.* 1972

Chopin, Kate (1851–1904). *Bayou Folk.* 1894

Stein, Gertrude (1874–1946). *Three Lives.* 1909

Faulkner, William (1897–1962). *Light in August.* 1932; *Absalom, Absalom!.* 1936

Stowe, Harriet Becher (1811–96). *Uncle Tom's Cabin.* 1852

Van Vechten, Carl (1880–1964). *Nigger Heaven.* 1926

Styron, William (1925–). *The Confessions of Nat Turner.* 1969

Wright, Richard (1908–60). *Native Son.* 1940

Ellison, Ralph (1914–). *Invisible Man.* 1952

Baldwin, James (1924–). *Go Tell it on the Mountain.* 1953; *Giovanni's Room.* 1956; *Another Country.* 1962

Purdy, James (1923–). *Malcolm.* 1959; *Cabot Wright Begins.* 1964; *Eustace Chisholm and the Works.* 1967

Capote, Truman (1924–). *Other Voices, Other Rooms.* 1948

Mailer, Norman (1923–). *Armies of the Night.* 1968; *Miami and the Siege of Chicago.* 1968

Roth, Henry (1906–). *Call it Sleep.* 1934

Fuchs, Daniel (1909–). *Summer in Williamsburg.* 1934; *Homage to Blenholt.* 1936; *Low Company.* 1937

Dahlberg, Edward (1900–). *Bottom Dogs.* 1929

West, Nathanael (1904–40). *The Dream Life of Balso Snell.* 1931; *Miss Lonelyhearts.* 1933; *A Cool Million.* 1934; *The Day of the Locust.* 1939

Fitzgerald, F. Scott (1896–1940). *The Last Tycoon.* 1941

Kafka, Franz (1883–1924). *The Trial.* trans W. and E. Muir, 1953

Roth, Philip (1933–). *Portnoy's Complaint.* 1969; *When She Was Good.* 1967; *The Breast.* 1973

Malamud, Bernard (1914–). *The Assistant.* 1957; *The Fixer.* 1967; *Pictures of Fidelman.* 1969

Solzhenitsyn. Alexander (1918–). *One Day in the Life of Ivan Denisovitch.* 1963, trans R. Parker, 1963

Bellow, Saul (1915–). *Dangling Man* 1944; *The Victim.* 1947; *The Adventures of Augie March.* 1953; *Henderson the Rain King.* 1959; *Herzog.* 1964; *Mr. Sammler's Planet.* 1969; *Humbolt's Gift.* 1973

Malcolm X (1925–65). *The Autobiography of Malcolm X.* (1965) (with Alex Haley)

Brown, Claude (1937–). *Manchild in the Promised Land.* 1965

CHAPTER 5: POPULAR FICTION

Pohl, Frederick (1919–) and Kornbluth, C. M. (1923–). *The Space Merchants.* 1953

Heinlein, Robert (1907–). *Stranger in a Strange Land.* 1969

Lawrence, D. H. (1885–1930). 'The Man Who Died', *Love Among the Haystacks And other Stories.* 1960

Vonnegut, Kurt (1922–). *Player Piano.* 1952; *The Sirens of Titan.* 1959; *Mother Night.* 1961; *Cat's Cradle.* 1963; *Slaughterhouse-Five.* 1965; *God Bless You, Mr. Rosewater.* 1965

Orwell, George (1903–50). *Nineteen Eighty-four.* 1949

Poe, Edgar Allan (1809–49). 'Murders in the Rue Morgue', in *The Prose Tales of Edgar Allan Poe.* 1843

Waugh, Hillary (1920–). *Last Seen Wearing . . . .* 1952

Hammett, Dashiell (1894–1961). *The Glass Key.* 1931; *Red Harvest.* 1929; *The Maltese Falcon.* 1930

Chandler, Raymond (1888–1959). *The Big Sleep.* 1939

Macdonald, Ross (1915–). *The Zebra-striped Hearse.* 1962; *The Far Side of the Dollar.* 1965

Millar, Margaret (1915–). *A Stranger in My Grave.* 1960; *Beyond this Point are Monsters.* 1970

Waugh, Evelyn (1903–66). *A Handful of Dust.* 1934

Highsmith, Patricia (1921–). *Strangers on a Train.* 1950; *Those who Walk Away.* 1967; *The Two Faces of January.* 1964

Blatty, W. P. (1928–). *The Exorcist.* 1971

Mitchell, Margaret (1900–49). *Gone With the Wind.* 1936

Herbert, Frank (1920–). *Dune.* 1965; *Dune Messiah.* 1969

Disch, Thomas M. (1940–). *Camp Concentration.* 1967

Bester, Alfred (1913–). *The Demolished Man.* 1953; *Tiger, Tiger.* 1956 (retitled *The Stars My Destination* for the US)

Delaney, Samuel R. (1942–). *Babel 17.* 1966; *The Einstein Intersection.* 1967

Le Guin, Ursula (1929–). *The Left Hand of Darkness.* 1969

Spinrad, Norman (1940–). *The Iron Dream.* 1973

CONCLUSION

Dos Passos, John (1896–1971). *USA.* 1938

Melville, Hermann (1819–91). *Moby Dick.* 1851

Fitzgerald, F. Scott (1896–1940). *The Last Tycoon.* 1941; *The Great Gatsby.* 1925

Index